Lost Souls: FOUND!™

Inspiring Stories About Northern-Breed Dogs

Kyla Duffy and Lowrey Mumford

Published by Happy Tails Books™, LLC

Happy Tails Books™ uses the power of storytelling to effect positive change in the lives of animals in need. The joy, hope, and (occasional) chaos these stories describe will make you laugh and cry as you em*bark* on a journey with these authors, who are guardians and/or fosters of rescued animals. "Reading for Rescue" with Happy Tails Books not only brings further awareness to animal advocacy efforts and breed characteristics, but each sale also results in a financial contribution to rescue efforts.

Lost Souls: Found!™ Inspiring Stories About Northern-Breed Dogs by Kyla Duffy and Lowrey Mumford

Published by Happy Tails Books™, LLC www.happytailsbooks.com

© Copyright 2012 Happy Tails Books™, LLC. Printed and bound in the United States of America. All Rights Reserved. No part of this book may be reproduced in any form or by any electronic or mechanical means, including information storage and retrieval systems, without written permission from the publisher.

The publisher gratefully acknowledges the numerous rescue groups and their members, who generously granted permission to use their stories and photos.

Any brand names mentioned in this book are registered trademarks and the property of their owners. The author and publishing company make no claims to them.

Photo Credits:

>Front: *Dylan*, Lisa Collings, http://www.lisabyrdphotography.com/
>Back Top: *Aurora*, Nancy Triggiani
>Right: Michael Witt, http://www.mikelwitt.com/
>Interior Title Page: Michael Witt, http://www.mikelwitt.com/
>Interior Introduction Page: *Cali & Ares*, Kathy Dewees

Publishers Cataloging In Publication Data Available Upon Request

ISBN: 978-0-9846801-7-7

Happy Tails Books appreciates all of the contributors and rescue groups whose thought-provoking stories make this book come to life.

Akita Rescue of Western New York (ARWNY)
http://www.Akitarescuewny.com/

Northern California Sleddog Rescue (NorSled)
http://www.NorSled.org/

Siberian Husky Rescue of Florida (SHRF)
http://www.siberrescue.com/

MUSH Rescue (Atlanta)
http://www.mushrescue.com/Huskyrescue/

St. Louis Samoyed Rescue
http://www.stlsamrescue.org/

Taysia Blue Siberian Husky Rescue
http://www.taysiablue.com/

Visit the following link for more information about the dogs, authors, and rescues featured in this book:

http://www.happytailsbooks.com/about/authors/

Table of Contents

INTRODUCTION: The Husky Effect vi

General Lee Conquers Georgia 13

Max Challenge, Max Reward 16

Cha-Ching! 19

Snake Germs 24

Northern Nibbles 28

Lesson in Grace 29

Who's in Charge? 32

Drastic Measures 35

Born, Not Made 37

Northern Nibbles 41

A Long Ways Away 42

Canine Cinderella 47

Dream Dog 51

Friends for Life 54

Northern Nibbles 60

Fostering Facts 61

Chillie's Warmth 64

Eight-Pack 69

Frenzied Furball 74

Nobody Knows 77

The ARWNY Seven (Plus Two!) 80

Northern Nibbles 85

Sleeping Beauty 86

Compañeros 90

Margun and the Wolf 93

Radiant Raki 97

Sometimes They Choose Us 102

Northern Nibbles 106

Feared and Fearful 107

Sister Sammys 111

Our Northern Light 114

Akita Angels 119

Déjà Vu 122

Northern Nibbles 126

Trauma Specialist 127

Winter Wonderland 130

Matchmaker 135

Pork Chop Pup 141

INTRODUCTION: The Husky Effect

The butterfly effect is a scientific theory that is often referenced in pop culture. It happens when many minor changes cause a major outcome, like the idea that the flittering wings of butterflies could have an effect on a weather event, like a tornado. In dog terms, it could be looked at as the shedding of hairs, one by one, having a significant effect on the baby birds in a cold climate, whose mom uses those hairs to build a nest that keeps them warm after they are born, thus giving them a better chance at life. For simplicity, let's call this the Husky effect.

I suppose it all started when I told my soon-to-be husband that I was a cat person and that I didn't want a dog. The only exception to this would be a Siberian Husky. (Don't ask – I have no idea why; I had just seen some as a kid and thought they were cool.) That was just my rule.

We started researching Siberian Huskies on the Internet to get an idea of what we were in for. We looked for hours and marveled at the differences in fur length, size, color, and eyes. Not knowing about rescue, we ended up buying our first Huskies, Badger and Jambalaya, 18 months apart, and I quickly fell in love with them.

Then we found a social networking site called Dogster, where we started communicating with Huskies from all over the globe (that's right: dogs, not people). Each dog had his own page and his own voice, though we did connect with some Husky-loving humans, too. From this, we learned the ins and outs of Husky ownership.

Husky effect #1: Learning to love dogs and connecting with Husky lovers like Nicole, Margie, Tesa, Sasha, and Tammi

At my job, I had the opportunity to work cross-functionally with another employee, and we hit it off immediately because we had dogs in common. He had just begun volunteering as a dog walker for the Nebraska Humane Society (NHS), and he encouraged me to volunteer also. Once I went through the training, I decided that I wanted to do adoption counseling. I was trained by some of the best volunteers any shelter could have.

Husky effect #2: Blasé Kris, Nancy, Chet, Nancy and Tim

I had just passed my training at NHS, but I still didn't really know my way around the building. One Saturday morning, I arrived earlier than usual, before it got busy. My new friend and trainer, Nancy, was there early, too. I mentioned to her that I had never really been in the back areas of the shelter, so she gave me a private tour.

Husky effect #3: Nancy

It was on that tour that I found Taysia Blue (formerly Princess). She was scheduled to be euthanized because she was old and not very healthy. When Mike and I made the decision to adopt her, we hadn't planned on such an education! We learned more than we ever dreamed: about integrating a non-socialized dog; about dog triggers, fighting, and calming signals; about managing energy.

We also learned that great dogs die every day in shelters – more than 13,700 – and about managing numbers in shelters. If a shelter has one available kennel to house a dog, they need to choose the most "adoptable," which certainly isn't a nine-year-old dog who gets dumped off for the third time and happens to have a seizure upon arrival.

Husky effect #4: Taysia Blue

Taysia Blue and my young female, Jambalaya, fought terribly almost every day. It was extremely stressful to keep the dogs separated. To help us work through the issues, our friend Roberta came over and made some suggestions. At that time, she also shared with me that she had always wanted to help rescue dogs, which I filed away in the back of my mind.

Husky effect #5: Roberta

Every day, when I looked at my sweet Taysia Blue, my heart ached knowing how close she had been to dying. I knew there was a need for a rescue but thought, "Someday."

Then, one day at work my phone rang. It was one of the receptionists from my vet's office calling about a family that "needed to get rid of" their seven-year-old, epileptic Husky. I called the family and heard their story. I temperament-tested the dog with my own dogs and networked until I was able to facilitate an adoption between the current owner and a new one! That was a great feeling.

Shortly thereafter, I got the next call. This was about a Husky who was out of time at a small-town animal control facility. They were supposed to have euthanized her a week earlier, but they just didn't have the heart. Now they were full and had no choice. The only thing I could do at this point was pick her up and take her to a safer place, where she would be evaluated and then put up for adoption. When I picked her up, the employees had prepared for me a clean dog with little, pink ribbons behind her ears. She looked adorable.

At the facility where I dropped her off as a "stray," she never made it to the shelter's adoption kennels, and I was never able to find out the whole story. I hope that a staff member or volunteer found her, fell in love, and adopted her.

Husky effect #6: Maya and the Husky with the pink bows

The need was becoming clear, so I retained a lawyer to help me with the paperwork and formed Taysia Blue Siberian Husky Rescue, a Nebraska non-profit corporation.

I started a Husky playgroup in order to meet other Husky enthusiasts who might be willing to assist with the rescue. I honestly thought we'd help about eight or ten Huskies that year. I contacted Roberta (Husky effect #5) and asked her to be on our board of directors. Tammi (from Husky effect #1) reached out and offered to help; she is now also a board member and is the leader of our Kansas City initiative.

Two years later, we continue to meet new Husky enthusiasts and are amazed by their compassion, commitment, and love for homeless Huskies. We never counted on making so many friends. The eight or ten Huskies I thought we'd save that first year turned out to number 47, which is largely due to the support of volunteers, friends, family members, and even some strangers, who occasionally leave a word of encouragement or share a happy story.

Husky effects #7, 8, 9…2,394,384: Volunteers, friends, and family who help to keep Taysia Blue Siberian Husky Rescue moving forward

All of the people who have helped along the way are like those flittering wings of butterflies, or the hairs falling from a dog, effectively altering the destructive path in which these defenseless, homeless animals have found themselves. Taysia Blue and the others thank you and beg you to keep "flapping your wings."

This book is full of stories from people who have been fortunate, like me, to be a part of "the Husky effect" (or "the Samoyed effect" or "the Akita effect"; call it whatever you'd like). I hope these stories penetrate your heart and soul like the hairs of our favorite breeds penetrate our carpets, car seats, and clothes, and that they lead you to greater love and compassion, and perhaps even to action, for animals in need. There are many ways to help, one of which is, of course, adoption. But even if you can't adopt, you can make a difference just by telling others about rescue and adoption, donating to your favorite organization, or taking some time out of your day to walk some dogs at your local shelter.

 *Jackie Roach*

Inspiring Stories About Northern-Breed Dogs

ARWNY Rescue Dogs Cali and Ares

"I rescued my first two Akitas in my 40s, and now Noelle in my 50s. I know I will rescue another Akita in my 60s, and I hope there will be another in my 70s (God willing). I hope I'll have the ability to rescue another in my 80s. And, after that, I hope someone rescues me. When the final door opens, I know I will see all my furry friends waiting for me. But of all the things I'm hoping for, the last one is just this: St. Peter, please will you let me sneak a really big box of doggie cookies through your gate?" - *Rick Young, ARWNY Adopter*

General Lee Conquers Georgia

How could I say no to saving General Robert E. Lee?

After all, my great, great, great-grandfather was a Confederate soldier with the Georgia Infantry, wounded at the Battle of Vicksburg and taken as a prisoner of war by the U.S. forces on July 4, 1863. On July 15, 1863, he signed terms of capitulation that he would not take up arms against U.S. forces and was paroled. He died a month later in a hospital in New Orleans, Louisiana.

I went to the shelter to pick up the "two- to three-year-old Husky" for MUSH Rescue and was presented with a dog who looked closer to seven, with a black tooth, a gash out of his snout, and more mats than a yoga class. We had been told by the shelter that his owner surrendered him "because of the downturn in the economy," but he looked more like the dog from *Homeward Bound* when he returned from his 2,000-mile journey. This dog had not been in a home in a long time.

The shelter handed over General Robert E. Lee's vet records along with his pedigree information. Who dumps a dog along with his papers? We learned that Lee, as we called him, was indeed a six-year-old, AKC-registered, purebred Siberian Husky. He was covered in ticks the size of Texas. They were so big that they would just fall out of his fur and die. I took him to the vet for a bath, and the reception people took pictures because they swore he was part wolf. Lee did not like being messed with and let you know by screaming. It wasn't a bark, and it wasn't a whine. This dog could scream!

Once home, Lee had no interest in his foster brothers and sisters and was even aggressive toward them. He just wanted to run free. We put him in an airline crate on wheels, and Lee moved the crate across the room in a matter of minutes. This dog was wilder than a bull at a rodeo! What had I gotten myself into? Over the years, we've fostered more than 60 dogs, but this one was a special challenge. The vet who neutered him had said that Lee would settle down around 90 days post-surgery, when the testosterone was out of his body. Could I hold out that long?

I looked for a home for Lee but worried about his safety because this dog could escape anything. I swear he opened my front door one day and let the other dogs out. They came back for a treat, while Lee played chase with my husband between two streets in the neighborhood until I could get there with chicken. The next time he escaped, he ran down the banks of the Chattahoochee with me in pursuit until I couldn't run anymore. I drove back to the area where he was last seen and found him standing by the road with a "Where have you been?" look on his face.

By the time we finally hit that 90-day mark, we had fallen hard for this furry ball of love, so we kept him.

Life with Lee has not settled down much. He recently got ahold of the kitchen sponge with the Brillo pad on one side and sponge on the other, and when I tried to take it, he swallowed it whole. I wrestled with him for about a half hour trying to get hydrogen peroxide down his throat, which, of course, ended up in my eye. We took him to the emergency vet, and they gave him something to make him throw it up. We knew it worked when we heard his scream. The vet came out with the whole sponge and the rest of his stomach contents!

This dog keeps us on our toes, but we wouldn't have it any other way. General Robert E. Lee may have helped conquer Mexico in the Mexican-American War, but General Robert E. Lee *the canine* has conquered our hearts!

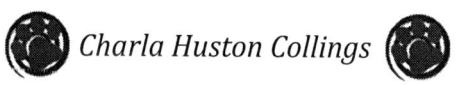
Charla Huston Collings

Max Challenge, Max Reward

Max, our first Samoyed, was a special boy. We adopted him when he was two years old. Max's upbringing was not a pleasant one. He had not been allowed indoors at his first home. As a result, Max had a lifelong fear of rain and thunderstorms. Adding to Max's trouble was the other dog living with him. With neither dog neutered, when Max reached maturity, the other dog began attacking him. The owner decided that he didn't want to deal with the problem, so he dumped Max at the pound.

Fortunately, Max found his way to Northern Illinois Samoyed Assistance (NISA), where he was cared for by a wonderful foster dad. Max needed to learn all the basics of in-home living, including housetraining, but one of his first lessons was about not *standing* on the dining room table!

We met Max on a lovely spring afternoon. For our three-year-old daughter, it was love at first sight. Our six-year-old American Eskimo Dog, Misty, wasn't as sure about Max during their first meeting, but they became instant friends the day we brought Max home, with constant "catch me if you can" games and wrestling matches.

Due to his poor living conditions, Max's coat was yellowish. After several weeks with us, his hair suddenly began to fall out in clumps. We were in a panic! We called the rescue group, fearful that Max had contracted a serious illness. Thankfully, nothing was amiss. We were relieved and a little embarrassed at our naivety to learn that Max would "blow" his coat twice yearly. With a healthy diet and comfortable environment, Max's coat went from yellow to brilliant white in a few months.

We knew Max was a sweetheart, but it was on a warm summer evening that we learned exactly how special he was. Max loved excursions, whether it was a walk in the park, a trip to a friend's house, or even a visit to the vet. My husband took Max along to his weekly softball games. He brought Max into the dugout with him, or asked one of the friends or family members of the players to keep him in the bleachers during the game. Max became the unofficial team mascot.

One evening, as my husband visited with teammates at the facility, a man approached and asked if his wheelchair-bound daughter, a young girl with cerebral palsy, could pet Max. Knowing Max's friendly demeanor, my husband agreed and walked Max closer to the girl so that she could reach him. Max moved slowly and gently laid his head in her lap, leaving it there for as long as she wanted to pet him. Max remained at the girl's side the entire evening.

One month later, at the softball facility, my husband saw a car drive by. Who was in the car? The mother of the girl with cerebral palsy, the father, their daughter, *and a Samoyed puppy.*

 *Susan Wheeler*

Cha-Ching!

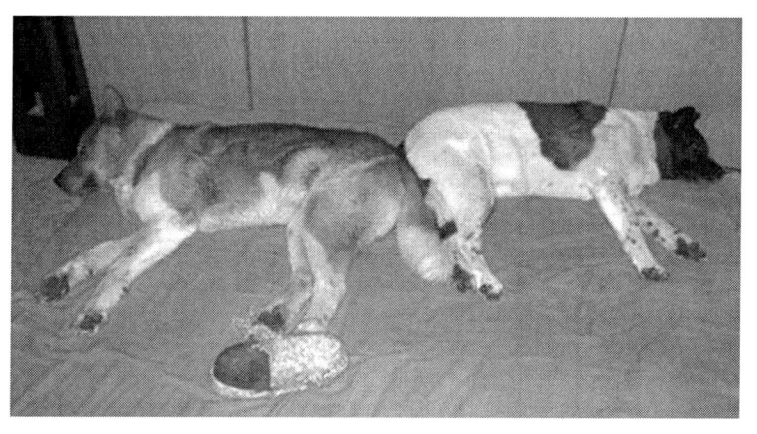

All Akita adoption contracts should read as follows:

Dear First-time Akita Adopter,

Before you take home your Akita, please understand that Akitas are like no other breed, and rescued Akitas are even more unique. You will soon realize it is you *being rescued today. After getting to know your Akita, you won't be able to say you have never hit the jackpot, or that you have not known what it is like to be truly rich. It won't be easy at first, but all the pain will be worth it, and you will never be the same again."*

If you agree, please sign here!

Where to start? When we drove from our home in Ontario to New York to adopt a pair of dogs, we met Kazan first. He was a mellow male who would happily sit quietly at your feet. Hannabee was a firecracker who couldn't sit still. Others had passed her over because they thought she was too hyper. We thought she just had plenty of love to share. My husband took Hannabee for a walk, and she looked right up at him. He rubbed his hand down her chest, and she went quiet. She let out a big sigh, and they bonded right then and there.

Kazan had come to Akita Rescue of Western New York (ARWNY) from Ohio. Hannabee was a six-month-old puppy who had been found in New Jersey. It was love at first sight for these two strays, so we took them both home with us.

Hannabee had cruciate ligament (knee) surgery at 10 months old. The vet said to keep her calm and keep the dogs separated for at least a few weeks. Oh, sure! (That was not happening.) We tried at first, but Hannabee twirled like a tornado in her crate when she heard Kazan howling outside. He sounded like a wolf with his paw in a trap. Thank God we live in the country, so neighbors probably just thought it was a wild animal. When I brought Kazan inside, they kissed through the crate, and he slept beside her. This went on for four months during her recovery.

Kazan developed thyroid problems, which required blood work twice a year. Every time I loaded him into the car, Hannabee cried. When we would return, Hannabee would perform a glorious dance and welcome Kazan with a special bark. The two would kiss and smell each other as though they had been separated for months!

This wasn't the only time the lovers were reunited. I was walking Kazan on a trail one winter day; Hannabee had already had her turn. I could hear her cry as we left for our walk, and then I turned back to see the shadow of a dog running toward us. It was her! She had climbed a snow pile in one corner of our yard and jumped over our five-foot fence. No problem! They were thrilled to see each other, and we all walked home together.

Hannabee is the queen; what is hers is hers, and what was Kazan's was also hers. Over the years, she stole more of his toys than I can count, and his only response was a tail wag.

As the years passed, Kazan didn't age well. He became sensitive to numerous foods, and his tummy often bothered him in the night. He always slept in the living room and paced when he was uncomfortable. Nurse Hannabee was charged with alerting "Doctor Mom." She would come to my side and wake me, urging me to check on Kazan. Kazan would paw me to let me know he wasn't feeling well, and I would take him outside to help him walk it off. Hannabee, of course, went back to bed; she had done her job. Kazan later settled well on grain-free food.

Then, Kazan's back end started to fail. He was sore and would move around to try to get comfortable. Sometimes he would come into our room for comfort. Hannabee would go to him and nudge him with her nose to get on her bed! The queen *never* gave up her bed for anyone, so this was a seriously loving gesture.

Finally, last year, things changed. My husband had just left and was 45 minutes away. Kazan seemed fine in the morning, but when I saw him outside eating grass, I began to worry. That was very unusual for him. Hannabee got my attention at the window from the fenced yard. When I ran toward her, Nurse Hannabee met me and led to Kazan. He wouldn't stop pawing me. He was bloating, and I knew it was time. My friend got us to the clinic, and we let him go.

I took Kazan home for his eternal rest that day. The drive was hard, but I owed it to him and Hannabee. She knew he left in a car, and she cried when I pulled back in. I took Kazan to the back of our property to bury him. Hannabee smelled him and licked his paw. She waited for him to move, but she understood; I know she did.

We had Kazan for seven short years, but for him, they were the best. He was happy until the end. When he passed, Hannabee seemed relieved that his suffering was over. When she makes her regular visits to his grave, she lies on it and seems happier afterward.

Though Kazan's time with us was too short, the lessons he taught us will last our lifetimes. Despite his health problems, Kazan was always happy to go anywhere and do anything. He worked within his limitations, never complaining and never looking at a challenge as a road block. He would just figure it out. He accepted things for what they were instead of wishing for what he wanted them to be, and he reminded us that today is all we have; tomorrow, if we get it, is a gift.

Hannabee continues Kazan's legacy by loving life to the fullest and clearly appreciating the simple things. When she lies on Kazan's grave, she reminds us that when you love someone, you do whatever it takes; you are there for them until the end.

So, back to the clause that should be added to Akita adoption contracts. We can never say that we haven't known what it is like to be truly rich. Caring for Hannabee, our silly puppy who loves life so much that she can't stay in her own skin, and Kazan, our quiet soul who forever kept us guessing, has been like hitting the jackpot. We will never be the same again; we will be *better* for the lessons they've taught us and the love they've shared with us. We can't wait to learn what our new Akita, Hachi, has to teach!

 *Janine & Troy*

Snake Germs

I am walking Taffy down the dead-end road early in the morning. The weeds are waist-high on both sides, except for a narrow mowed strip. Unlike his usual self, Taff is toddling along and sniffing the ground all over like a herd of Buffalo has just passed.

On the way back, Taffy is actually lagging behind, so I tell him to come on. Suddenly, he bounds by me like a race car, does a 45-degree turn, and pounces in the high weeds on the uphill side of us like a lightning strike, going clear to the end of his 30-foot lead and almost pulling my arm out of the socket! I hear a LOUD crash, and I panic. Oh, don't let it be a skunk!

Out of the tall weeds comes Taff, thrashing like a fish out of water. Wrapped completely around his head is the biggest *snake* I've ever seen! Oh. My. God.

Now Taff is frantically shaking his head, which is the very thing his eye doctor specifically warned me not to let him do after his recent cataract surgery. The snake has its head inches from Taff's repaired eye, and Taff is flinging it up and down, back and forth. The snake's tail is whipping in the air like a bull whip and slamming on the road with a loud crack each time Taff shakes it.

I am in a complete state of panic. I run clear to the end of his lead and yell at the top of my lungs, "Drop it! Stop shaking!"

Taff actually stops, and the snake tries to bite his newly-repaired eye, of course. I scream louder, "Kill it! Drop it! Stop shaking! Shake its brains out! Get that thing off your head right now!"

I'm nonsensical, and Taff is totally ignoring me as the snake wraps itself around his head more tightly. I am 30 feet away and not wearing my glasses, so I have no idea what kind of snake it is, but I can make out big diamonds on the snake's back. If you think for a second I am going to get closer to see the head and/or ask for identification to see if it is poisonous, you are sorely mistaken.

I am not a huge fan of snakes, and those diamonds are making me nervous. The thing is as big around as my leg and surely about 75 feet long! I'm at a total loss as to what to do, so I break into a flat-out run down the road, dragging Taff, who is still shaking his head to fling off the snake. I keep jerking on the long lead because I'm moving so fast. Trust me, when being followed by a snake-wrapped dog, you would suddenly become a marathon winner, too. My intention is to drag him and the snake back to "Dad," who is way past due to handle a Taff stunt anyway!

I keep jerking Taff's lead and looking back over my shoulder. Suddenly, Taff drops the snake, so I leap ahead like a racehorse out of the gate at the Kentucky Derby. Taff digs in his big paws and tries to stop me; it becomes a tug of war between me and a big, 65-pound, white dog, with a slithering, dizzy, slimy snake in between us. Yikes! The snake is slowly uncoiling completely across the road. It looks like a fire hose. Taff clears the snake in one leap before it lifts its head. I lose all sense of sanity and scream, "Run!"

But Taff doesn't want to run. Instead, he continues to literally dig his claws into the blacktop. He jerks his lead as hard as he can. Now, Taff is strong, but I have *lots* of adrenalin on my side and a rearing black *anaconda* (surely it was!) to help things along. I have no idea how fast a snake can move, but, trust me, I can move faster, even if I have to drag Taff.

Down the road I race, and Taff finally decides to catch up. He is panting with tongue lolling out, and my heart is about to stop because I'm completely sure he has been bitten and is going to go into death throes any minute. I forget about the full-blown, muscle-ripping tug-of-war I've just won, and we charge three-quarters of a mile down the road in the 90-degree, hot, humid air.

When I get to the house, I burst in, chugging like a steam engine. I start washing Taff's eye out with saline but then decide that it would be best to wash his whole face. I check every inch of his face and neck and shoulders for bite marks, but Taff is in wrestle-mode. Despite his fighting me, I pin him to the floor and scream, "You stupid idiot! What were you thinking? That snake could have killed you! Even if it wasn't poisonous, *it could have bit out your $2500 eye!*"

My husband is now with me, assuring me that if the snake had bitten him, Taff would have cried out. He is convinced by my description that it was a plain ole' black snake, more of a constrictor than a biter. He brings up some pictures on the computer, and sure enough, that is what it was. He still doesn't believe my description of its size.

"Yeah," I tell him. "Well, you just go down there and look at the slime trail clear across the road. I'm tellin' ya, it was GIGANTIC. I couldn't see Taff's face at all. It was a nightmare. I don't even know how he could *breathe*!"

Then, I scream even louder at Taff, "See! A *constrictor*. It could have cut off the blood to your eye; it could have squeezed you so tightly that it popped out *both* eyes. What were you thinking? Hold still; let me check your teeth. Ewww. Snake germs in your mouth."

I flush it with saline, too.

I finally manage to convince myself that Taff has no bite marks or snake germs left on him anywhere, and apparently the violent head shaking has not hurt his optic nerve. He continues to give me the *evil* eye, which is *not* what we'd had in mind when we paid a small fortune to get his eye fixed!

I have no idea how he knew that snake was there, went airborne, and pounced 30 feet through the thick brush to grab it with one strike. Obviously, his eyes and ears both work just fine.

It makes my skin crawl just to type this. That's it with the long-lead walkin', yesiree bob!

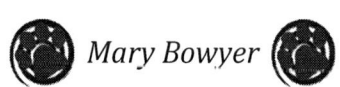

Mary Bowyer

Northern Nibbles

Training Triumph: On a warm summer day, we adopted Chilly, a beautiful, deep-red Husky, who sat quietly in his cage at the adoption fair amidst many other barking dogs. During the first few months, Chilly didn't realize he had found his permanent home and suffered some separation anxiety. Additionally, feeding him was like opening the doors to the mall on Black Friday. If he didn't manage to knock the bowl out of our hands, he inhaled the kibble so fast that we were sure he would choke. He was equally as voracious on our walks and knew where all the cherry trees were. Chilly put his extreme food motivation to work and learned in a day that if he sat and waited until the bowl was in place, he got to eat. His separation anxiety has now disappeared, and as for mealtimes, we can even leave him alone with his food, and he won't eat until we give him the command. -*Heidi Ferguson*

Handsome Little Devils: I have been volunteering with Husky rescue for more than a decade, ever since I adopted my Husky, Keno. Huskies are known to be quite the difficult breed. Once you get over the gorgeous looks and those ice-blue eyes, you often find out that they are little monsters (handsome ones)! I say that with the utmost fondness, as I have fostered more than 10 of them throughout the years, and they are what I call *unique*. They act like two-year-olds most of the time, but that is part of their charm! -*Simone Kuska*

Lesson in Grace

I adopted Arwen from Northern California Sled Dog Rescue (NorSled) six years ago. They had pulled her from a shelter and provided her with care after she had been hit by a car and severely wounded. Though her leg was beyond saving and had to be amputated, Arwen was (and still is) a beautiful, silver-and-white Siberian Husky with gorgeous blue eyes. At the time, she was shy and fearful, which is why people had passed her by for many months. I met her at a pet fair and was moved by her story and her beauty. Having a quiet house with two mellow dogs, I knew I could provide her with a forever home in which she would thrive.

When her foster mom brought her to my house, Arwen picked up a dog toy to play with. Her foster mom said it was the first time she had seen Arwen act like a normal dog. I knew then that we had found each other for a reason. Her blue eyes and silver fur inspired me to name her Arwen, after the Elvish character from Lord of the Rings. She settled in quickly with the other dogs and soon felt at home. (In true Husky style, she proceeded to chew the arms of two chairs.) She remained shy with other people, but we bonded quickly.

Early the following spring, I noticed that Arwen's bottom gums were growing in-between her teeth. My veterinarian operated to remove what was believed to be a benign growth. Within a few weeks, her gums had begun to grow back, so we were referred to a specialist and scheduled to have a portion of her bottom jaw removed. After the first operation, I received the dreaded late-night call from the veterinarian telling me that the biopsy on the jaw bone indicated that Arwen had a rare cancer, and that the protocol for that cancer was to take even more of the jaw. In total, about 25% of her bottom jaw was removed.

My poor girl was losing body parts at an alarming rate! After a third operation, the biopsy report was thankfully clear, but Arwen was still a long way from a full recovery. She was not supposed to chew, so for the next six weeks she ate dog food ground into a paste. Luckily, her jaw healed, and she has been fine since. You cannot even see that she is missing any of her bottom jaw unless you know to specifically look for it.

When I first adopted Arwen, I thought of her as a handicapped dog because of the loss of her leg. But even after the partial removal of her jaw, it is evident that Arwen certainly does not see herself as less than whole. She welcomes life enthusiastically, as though nothing were missing. Her happiness and her activities are in no way affected by her missing parts. She loves to run and take long walks. The only accommodation she needs is a boost to jump up on the bed. I no longer think of her as handicapped.

During her ordeal with jaw cancer, I was struck by Arwen's patience and quiet acceptance of the care she was receiving. She has remained shy of most people and is particularly uncomfortable around men, but she calmly endured all the exams and treatments, as if she knew that the veterinarians were helping her. They even commented on her gentle nature.

I look at Arwen's response to her troubles as a lesson in grace. During the time that Arwen was ill, a close family member was also facing a life-threatening illness. It was Arwen's example that helped me through that time and taught me how to accept with grace what life deals to us.

It has been five years now since Arwen's illness, and she is still a healthy, happy girl. She now shares her home with two female Huskies and a male Hound-mix. I'm sure she would prefer to be the only dog, but having the other dogs around doesn't change that fact that Arwen and I share a special bond. All I have to do is say her name, and she happily wags her tail. She quietly comes to lie near me when I am feeling sad or upset, wanting nothing more than to comfort me. Arwen is slowly but surely becoming more comfortable with other people. Best of all, my "disabled" dog has "enabled" me to see things in a whole new way.

Tricia Wintch

Who's in Charge?

When Reo (short for "Oreo") died suddenly of a brain tumor, the dog love in our home was depleted by one-third. Reo was a Malamute/Bernese Mountain Dog-mix (we suppose), and Tim and I had both had Alaskan Malamutes before we met, so we had a soft spot for the breed. We searched Petfinder.com and found a four-year-old male named Dakota. The rescue told us that he had been abandoned by a breeder because "he didn't look enough like a Malamute." He was several hundred miles away in St. Louis, but Tim was planning a trip to St. Louis anyway, so we decided to seriously look into adopting him.

We filled out the application, and the rescue went through the usual screening process. They wanted to know about our experience with Malamutes and contacted our vet for a reference.

The day before Tim was to leave St. Louis, he went to meet Dakota. The people at the rescue had brought him to their house in the city from the kennel in an outlying area. As soon as he was released from an upstairs room, Dakota bounded down the stairs, really excited, it seemed, to be running around loose. He approached Tim right away and presented his belly to be rubbed. Dakota seemed to be the "big teddy bear" that the rescue had described.

Tim and Dakota spent the night in our old house in St. Louis. Dakota seemed like a typical dog. He slept by the door, presumably guarding it against intruders. On the return trip, Tim turned onto a state highway, and Dakota started barking madly, as though he had some horrible recollection of the open field they were passing.

When Dakota arrived home, he took a casual interest in me and the other dogs. He seemed a bit aloof at first, and then he began demonstrating some signs of aggression. As I was lying on the floor next to him, just petting his head, he growled at me. And although he was pleased to go into his crate for the night, when the other dogs approached it, he started running wildly in circles, growling and barking. The next day brought more of the same.

I was terrified that Dakota would hurt Maggie, our elderly German Shepherd. Having just lost Reo, I was overwhelmed with fear and anxiety about Maggie – overwhelmed to the point of irrationality. I am ashamed to say it, but I wanted to return Dakota to the rescue.

I told my friend Jason about Dakota, and he came to meet him. When Jason arrived and sat down, Dakota approached him in a friendly way and allowed Jason to pet him. Dakota seemed more relaxed than he had before.

Jason suggested that Dakota perceived our grief as weakness and that he was simply stepping into the alpha role, a job that he perceived as vacant. All we needed to do was to put aside our grief and exude the strength of spirit that an alpha dog should possess.

We did just that. There was no need to "correct" or directly modify Dakota's behavior; we simply cast aside our feelings of vulnerability, and Dakota started radiating the sweet spirit that Malamutes typically possess. He became a joyous, gentle dog who has never met a stranger. He even greets the vet with big smile, a wagging tail, and his signature greeting, "Woo woo woo woo woo woo woo!"

While Dakota knows that he is not the alpha dog, he assumes a leadership role in our family by serving as big brother to his younger sisters; when the girls came to us as traumatized rescue puppies, Dakota made them feel safe and showed them what it means to be part of a family.

Charlotte Grider

Drastic Measures

I was reading my emails, and one from Sibernet-L, a Siberian-interest mailing list, caught my eye. It was about a six-month-old Siberian Husky puppy, who had been turned in to a kill shelter after suffering a broken tail and two breaks to her pelvis.

The owners had waited five days before surrendering her and hadn't provided her with any medical care. She could not walk or control her bowels and bladder. Husky House rescued her and took her to their vet, who recommended euthanasia. The rescuers struggled with this and decided to take a night to sleep on it. In the meantime, I kept looking at her picture and seeing a beautiful, little, blue-eyed, red-and-white girl, who seemed to be begging, "Please help me! I want to live."

It broke my heart to think of this stunning young puppy being put down, so I emailed Lorraine at Husky House and asked her to please not have the puppy euthanized; we would adopt her just as she was. Our family had experience with special-needs dogs like this, and we wanted to help this puppy have at least a few good years. Lorraine agreed and made arrangements for transport. She also said she would ask the vet to repair her pelvis to give her a chance to walk again.

The next morning, Lorraine called and said Aiyana (the name we gave her, which means "forever blossoming flower" in Inuit) was up and walking, drinking, and peeing on her own! I think the medicines they gave her for pain had really helped her. We drove from our home in Tennessee to Kentucky to pick her up from a transport volunteer and take her home.

Aiyana is now a healthy and happy two-year-old. She loves life and plays for hours with our black, male Labrador Retriever. She does everything any other Husky can do, like run in the back yard and play in her pool. The only reminder of her injury is that she cannot raise her tail above her back. That is fine with us, much better than the original prognosis, which was that it would have to be amputated!

We are glad we decided to give her a chance! She is our Aiyana, our Blossoming Flower, our sweet, loving Siberian Husky girl, who has forever placed her paw prints deep in our hearts.

 *Brenda & Bob Weddle*

Born, Not Made

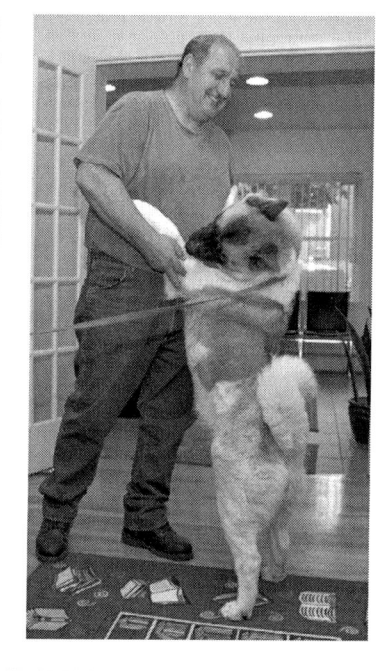

Apple, a 4½-year-old Akita, came to live with me after several other families had given her up. After the first night of crying by the back door, she accompanied me to my office, where she met Antonio, a co-worker who was suffering through the loss of his father and his wife's battle with cancer. Apple ran right up to him and stood on her hind legs, wiggling around and trying to kiss his face. Despite his sadness, Antonio smiled. That's when I first noticed Apple's uncanny ability to relate to people in emotional need.

For the next few months, as Apple again adjusted to life at a new home, she never failed to make Antonio grin when she came to work with me on Fridays. During this time, I researched what it would take to register Apple as a therapy dog. I wasn't sure if her age or lack of training would hold her back, but I found out that taking an AKC Canine Good Citizen (CGC) course was a beginning. The CGC requires ten tasks that are needed for therapy dog certification. Apple would then have to learn four additional skills: not reacting to medical equipment, such as a cane, walker, or wheelchair; visiting with a person in a wheelchair or bed; not reacting to physical infirmities, such as an uneven gait or heavy breathing; and responding immediately to the "leave it" command, which can be especially challenging in cases where food has been dropped on the floor.

We took the CGC course, and she excelled. (It turned out that it wasn't really Apple who needed the training; it was me!) The CGC instructor's Corgis were certified for therapy work by Therapy Dogs International (TDI), and she encouraged us to do the same. I researched it and liked what the TDI website had to say: "TDI registration is a natural extension of the AKC CGC for dogs who are particularly sensitive and attentive to people." The organization had the philosophy that a therapy dog is born, not made. It looked like a perfect fit for Apple and me, and before the end of the summer, we had passed the TDI tests and begun weekly visits at a rehabilitation hospital and a nursing home.

The next year we added two other nursing homes, and then we got involved with several children's reading programs. These programs provide a relaxed atmosphere where students can practice their reading skills without feeling judged. Both their reading and their self-esteem usually improve.

We did a pre-reading program with three- to five-year-olds and were able to link up with several library programs, including one called "Martha Speaks Aloud Book Club," which is based on the public television series in which a rescued dog eats vegetable soup with pasta letters in it and then learns to speak. This program helps children learn to interact safely with dogs and encourages empathy. For example, one session called "Not Afraid of Dogs" teaches children how to safely approach and pet a dog.

Apple truly excels at comforting people of all ages. One of the places we visit regularly is Jewish Nursing Home (JNH), where we used to be greeted at the door on Sunday mornings by Sarah, a feisty, tiny woman in her 80s who powered around the nursing home in a bright blue scooter-wheelchair. Every week Apple and I sat by Sarah's side, as she told us tales of her beloved home, Budapest. We learned that Sarah had private tutors growing up, and that before World War II broke out in Hungary, she was a child actress and dancer. Sarah lost her entire family, more than 30 people, to the Holocaust. In 1945, she immigrated by foot to the Austrian border and then to Vienna. She had lived everywhere, from Israel to Springfield, Massachusetts. Sarah was a survivor.

Sarah loved to sit outside and stroke Apple's head, at one point, telling me that doing so was like the warmth of the sun. In her room, Sarah had enlarged pictures and murals of her dogs. She loved to talk about them.

One October day, Sarah asked if I could take a picture of her with Apple. She told Apple to "place," and immediately

Apple put her head on Sarah's knee. I snapped a few shots with my phone. I later made prints of them and framed one for Sarah. She kept it on the small refrigerator in her room.

Months later Sarah fell ill and eventually died. At her funeral service, I realized how much I had learned from this survivor and how much knowing her had added to my life. TDI, and, more specifically, Apple, had been the mechanism that brought us together. Apple is nothing short of a gift, and it's hard to believe that her previous humans were too blind to see that. Although Apple's families had given up on her, she never gave up on loving people.

The picture of Sarah and Apple may have been the very last picture taken of Sarah. It was the photograph used for her online obituary, and it is an image I keep close to my heart.

 *Judith Kelly*

Northern Nibbles

Good Use: Samoyeds blow their coats twice a year, which equals lots of fur everywhere! After sweeping up piles of fluffy dog hair from my adopted Samoyeds, Murphy and Connor, I started twisting their fur and learning to spin it into yarn, as some Russian women do. Spinning lessons taught me how to create a wonderful, soft yarn that feels like cashmere. Now, with several spinning wheels, I can spin Murphy's and Connor's fur and the fur of other Samoyeds into yarn that has become hats, scarves, and mittens. These items are a great way to remember pets who have passed on, and they also make wonderful fundraising items for St. Louis Samoyed Rescue. -*Suzanne E. Devaney*

Hope Springs Eternal: Just a couple of days after I started volunteering with Taysia Blue Siberian Husky Rescue, I received my first foster dog. Having two wonderful Huskies of my own, I couldn't wait to help other Huskies who weren't as lucky as ours. Hope was a sad-looking, 18-month-old Husky whose time had run out at the shelter. The poor thing had already had a litter of puppies and three homes that we knew of. Her coat was thin and dirty, and all she wanted was belly rubs. Applications to adopt her came in, but we were already smitten, so we ended up adopting her ourselves. With our little princess home for good, we feel like a complete family. -*Stephanie Konz*

A Long Ways Away

A lot of rescue groups refer to the Gandhi quote, "The greatness of a nation and its moral progress can be judged by the way its animals are treated."

We are definitely headed in the wrong direction.

I had heard of animal rescue groups but didn't know much about them. I was most aware of Greyhound rescues because I assumed that the need for them directly resulted from breeding for the racing industry. I had no idea that there were rescues for any and all breeds.

I had lived in this state of blissful ignorance until the lovely Lesa came into my life. Lesa was acutely aware of the extent of the homeless pet problem and opened my eyes to it. I was horrified.

Huskies have always held a special place in my heart. They are absolutely wonderful dogs. They require a ton of exercise and shed a lot of hair, but if you are up for the walks and think being covered in dog hair is fashionable, then they might be the dogs for you.

When I was laid off last February, I decided to spend some of my newfound freedom helping out, so I did some research and found a Husky rescue in St. Petersburg, Florida. I know what you are thinking: "A Husky? In Florida?"

They are indeed here, and they do surprisingly well in the heat and humidity. Their extra coat protects them from the heat, just like it does from the cold, and it keeps the sun off of their sensitive skin.

I applied to be a short-term foster parent for Siberian Husky Rescue of Florida (SHRF). Lesa and I were discussing moving in together, and because she had Oreo, a 15-year-old, declawed, deaf, arthritic cat, there was simply no way we could think of bringing a young, prey-driven Husky into the house. It simply wasn't fair to Oreo. Therefore, we had to be a little picky about which Huskies came to stay with us.

Servo arrived in March, approximately a week after my volunteer application was approved. I was told that Servo was rescued from the streets of Tampa along with a female Husky. The female was microchipped and was returned to her guardians somewhere in West Virginia. How she came to Tampa is anyone's guess. Someone speculated that she may have been stolen and brought to Tampa, where she and Servo hooked up and later escaped their captors. I think it's possible that both Servo and the female actually walked to Florida from West Virginia. However he got here, Servo was suddenly alone and in the custody of the Hillsborough County Animal Control.

When I met him, Servo was a shadow of what he should have been, weighing in at a mere 51 pounds when he should have been 70 pounds. SHRF was called, and after the requisite veterinary examination and neutering, Servo was picked up by his initial foster mother.

You are probably wondering about his name. His first foster mother gave it to him, as it is the Latin word for "saved." The correct pronunciation is *ser-wo*, but that is just too dorky for such a cool dog, so we pronounce the "vee" instead.

His first foster mother had two small children visiting, so SHRF asked if we could take Servo for a couple of weeks while her guests were in town. He was being fostered south of St. Petersburg, so we drove down and picked him up. He was a little scared and defensive, but we soon got him to hop into my Jeep, and away we went. We had to stop by Lesa's place to take care of Oreo, so while Lesa did that, I took Servo for our first walk together. He didn't seem to know what to do or how to act; he was all over the place.

Eventually, we made it to my place and attempted to get Servo settled in. The first night was a little rough, as he had diarrhea and threw up twice, expelling what appeared to be a T-shirt he had eaten somewhere. No exaggeration. I've never seen a piece of material so big, and I'm still astonished it came from his stomach.

    I am convinced that it was at that precise moment that Servo hatched his plan to work his way into our hearts, and he executed it beautifully. We began our daily ritual of walks in the morning, before dinner, and before bed. Servo had magically learned to walk on a leash while he was sleeping and has been great ever since. (Many Huskies pull on their leashes because they think you are the sled they are genetically trained to pull.) Servo never tried to get on any furniture and never chewed a thing.

    The two weeks were fast coming to a close, and Lesa began hinting that we should call SHRF and see if we could keep Servo longer. I made the call, and they said that they would be happy to let us become his full-time foster parents. It would be especially beneficial for Servo since his initial foster mother lived outside of town, and she had a hard time getting him to adoption events, which significantly limited his prospects.

    We began taking him to these events. I vividly remember looking up at Lesa at one event when I put the "adopt me" sign around Servo's neck. She was practically in tears. We began talking about ways we could adopt him ourselves, but when we tried to introduce Servo to Oreo, we only had limited success. Poor Oreo's heart beat like crazy as soon as he saw Servo. It just didn't seem like it would work.

    We kept taking Servo to adoption events. There were two potential adopters who stepped forward. As Servo's foster parents, we had the final say on which home we thought would be a good environment for him, and we found that both situations had issues that made them less than ideal. Looking back on it now, no one could have met the bar we set for Servo. Had we cloned ourselves, we probably would have found fault and not given him up.

Fate intervened one very sad morning when Oreo passed away. Fortunately, Lesa was there with him when he passed, and he was at home. He was spared the agony of an illness that might have made his last days painful, and we were spared the agony of euthanizing him. We were also spared the grief of having to give up Servo. We are hopeful that, at some point in the future, we will be able to introduce a cat into our family, but for now, it is just the three of us.

I don't think Servo ever had a real puppyhood, so he never learned to play with toys like the ones we bought him. He is slowly learning how to do it, and we are delighting in helping him to learn what the "good life" is like.

To go back to my initial comment about the Gandhi quote, it would be more accurate to say that we are not *all* headed in the wrong direction. While, as a whole, we may still be as far away from solving the problem of pet overpopulation as Servo was from our home when his journey began, because of the people who make up great organizations like SHRF, there is certainly hope.

 Rob Taylor

Canine Cinderella

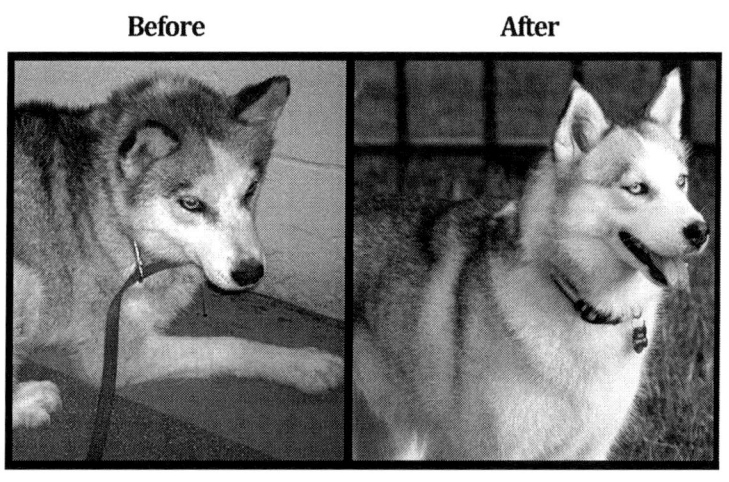

Before | After

Sheba was born in a Georgia puppy mill. The owners kept her in deplorable conditions and bred her again and again for three years before the puppy mill was shut down and the owners prosecuted for animal cruelty. If not for the brave actions of a young woman who recorded the conditions on her cell phone camera and contacted the authorities, Sheba might still be trapped in that puppy mill.

Siberian Husky Rescue of Florida (SHRF) rescued Sheba, the small, 30-pound, white-and-beige Husky, along with other Huskies, and asked us if we could foster her. They felt we were her last hope because she was showing signs of aggression and was obviously terrified, mostly hiding in the back of her crate. She needed a quiet environment where she could come to feel safe in order to begin the recovery process and learn to trust humans.

In my first meeting with her, I saw the fear in Sheba's eyes. Her spirit seemed broken, and her thick coat was stained red from the Georgia clay. She immediately went to a dark corner, where she stayed for hours at a time only to move from there to the security of her crate. In an effort to show her that she was safe, I regularly sat near her, spoke softly, and tried not to make any sudden movements. Sheba tensed up and hugged the wall whenever I touched her, as if it were painful. I couldn't approach her head-on; I had to ease up to her from the side and let the first move be hers. This went on for weeks with progress coming very slowly.

Sheba hardly ate anything at all during mealtimes. I hand-fed her one piece of food at a time until she had eaten her fill. She drank water so fast and intensely that she choked, so I put water in three different places around the house to help her understand that water would be readily available. When I offered her treats, Sheba took each one very softly and with great hesitation, as if she feared it was trap, and then she would run to a corner and hide with the treat under her chin. She broke treats into many pieces and slowly ate each one (which she still does to this day, savoring each morsel).

The first break came one day when I was in the bathroom. As I sat there "reading," Sheba gently pushed the door open, walked over, and softly laid her head in my lap. I can only assume that she felt comfortable because I was at her level and wasn't seeking anything from her.

I will never forget taking her for our first walk. Sheba's eyes lit up; she jumped for joy, spun around in circles, and almost went out of control. Connecting the leash to her collar was certainly a challenge, but I didn't mind because she was excited, not afraid. Those walks were the beginning of the daily ritual she needed. Every morning, she looked forward to her walk, staring at me as I had my morning coffee, as if to say, "Drink up and let's go!"

Our first trip to the dog park was amazing. I have never seen a dog's eyes so bright and a smile so big. Sheba hopped like bunny and ran so freely that it made my heart sing. Time at the park is her ultimate freedom, and she enjoys every second of it.

In addition to patience at home and frequent outings to "fun" places, our other adopted Husky, Kiva, was a big part of Sheba's adjustment. She seemed to know that Sheba needed a friend and playmate as she settled into her new home, and she gave Sheba just that.

Slowly, I began to realize that the best part of my day was seeing Sheba smile, watching her bask in the sun, and knowing that she finally felt safe and comfortable. Though Sheba had been dealt a bad hand, she responded with courage, for which we were both rewarded. She began waking every morning with a smile and kisses for everyone. Joy filled her eyes, and a song filled her voice. At mealtime, she would get so excited that she would spin around and around as I brought out her food. From a troubled dog nobody would have wanted to a perfect little princess, what a transformation Sheba had undergone!

After all the love, patience, time, and dedication I had invested in Sheba, I received the call that every foster parent knows eventually will come and usually welcomes: SHRF had someone who wanted to adopt Sheba. We had fostered many Huskies before and were always happy when they found their forever homes, but this time was different. Sheba had captured my heart, and I just couldn't let her go.

Terri Rodawald

Dream Dog

The story of Ivan actually begins with another Husky, Boris, who was my search and rescue partner for several years. We went on numerous search missions together. Boris passed away at the age of 15, about six months before Ivan came into my life. The night before I found Ivan online, Boris came to me in a dream and told me it was my turn to search... Our final search and rescue mission was to find Ivan. The next day I went onto Petfinder.com, and there was Ivan, sitting on the concrete floor of a gray, state-run shelter, smiling back at me. I knew he was the one; I had to complete my "mission" and adopt him from the kill shelter near Atlanta, Georgia.

The next day I went to meet him. I took my wife's Husky, Luna, with me, as it was important that Luna and Ivan get along. The officers brought Ivan out to the small, fenced area next to the building. He barked at Luna a few times and then picked up a rubber bone and began to play with her. They hit it off as if they were old friends! I was thrilled, though I had yet to see how he would interact with me. I sat on a bench in the fenced area and let him come to me. He greeted me by sitting between my legs and leaning back against me, as if to say, "I knew you'd come for me! I'm ready to go home now."

My heart melted, and I was sure this dog was meant for me. I called my wife and told her that we had to adopt him, no matter what.

We waited anxiously for several days for the shelter to call us to say that Ivan was ready for adoption. When that day finally came, I packed up the whole family (the wife, Luna, and me) and headed to the shelter. When we arrived, they informed us that Ivan was heartworm-positive and asked if we still wanted to adopt him. My heart broke for him, knowing that if we said no, he would most likely be put down. I looked at my wife and saw in her eyes that she agreed we had to do whatever we could to save him. We understood it would be a hard road for him (for all of us, really), but we knew in our hearts that we had to try.

The treatment was very tough, with shots on both sides of Ivan's lower back on multiple occasions. It looked like someone had shoved baseballs under his fur. Ivan was miserable, cranky, and lonely during the mandatory eight-week isolation from Luna and from play in general. We felt so helpless, as there was nothing we could do for him but wait. On top of that, there was no guarantee that the "cure" wouldn't do him more harm than the heartworms. Time dragged on; it seemed like forever.

It's been a little over a year now since we brought Ivan home. He has recovered from the heartworms and the treatment to become a healthy, happy, loving, well-adjusted Husky who completes our pack. His favorite toy is still the rubber bone (just like the one he had played with at the shelter), and he and Luna are inseparable. I never doubted that he was meant to be a part of our family and am so thankful to Boris for bringing all of us together.

I haven't dreamed of Boris since that night (which seems so long ago), but I know he's proud, and I know he is with us, looking over our pack, keeping us safe.

 *Mark Craig*

Friends for Life

The second time I met Jenny, she put both front paws on my shoulders, and we hugged. She remembered me! We were thrilled to see each other again.

The saga that led to our happy embrace began with a friend's daughter, Pattie, who is a veterinary technician. She knew I wanted a playmate for my Norwegian Elkhound/Chow-mix, Buddy. He was home while I was at work, but in the evenings and on weekends, we went for walks in the big city park behind my back fence. When my medical condition worsened, I became unable to walk him, so I needed a "buddy" to keep Buddy entertained.

Two Siberian Huskies, Silver and Jenny, had just been surrendered to the veterinarian's office where Pattie worked. The owner was tired of having to board them when traveling and of tracking them down when they escaped through his fence. Pattie knew Jenny was a sweetheart and encouraged me to adopt her.

Having no experience with Siberians, I learned from the Internet that they require a lot of exercise and can get bored and destructive without it. I also found out that they are escape artists and can make your yard look like the beach after the Normandy invasion! That didn't sound like a good fit for me: I wouldn't be able to be Jenny's running partner or even go after her if she dug her way out of the yard – the yard I'd been working on to create a flower-filled outdoor room.

Nevertheless, one Sunday Pattie drove me to Jacquie's house, where Jenny was staying with several other Siberian Huskies, all awaiting adoption through Bay Area Siberian Husky Rescue and Referral (BASH). Upon meeting Jenny, I loved her snowy-white face, ice-blue eyes with heavy black "eyeliner," and cute, white nose with black "freckles." Our meeting flew by, and before I knew it, Pattie was driving Jenny and me home! (Apparently the pen is mightier than both the sword *and* the Internet, as I put my signature on Jenny's adoption paperwork despite my concerns about the information I had gathered.)

Jenny was a little standoffish at first, but that was to be expected. I made sure that she knew where the dog door was and kept an eye on her as she explored her new surroundings. That first night, Buddy and I slept on my bed as usual, and Jenny slept in my bedroom on a large dog bed that Buddy had never used. I put a baby gate across the doorway as a precaution.

Monday was a business holiday, but I had a dental appointment that morning. I got up, put the coffee on, and let Buddy and Jenny out into the back yard through the sliding door in the family room. A minute later I checked that the two dogs were okay, and they were – just sniffing around the large palm tree that housed many squirrels. I checked again a few moments later, and everything was okay. On the third check, Buddy was there, but Jenny was gone!

I rushed to the living room in time to see her loitering in the front yard of the house across the street, but when I went outside and called for her, she turned and trotted around the corner toward the park! My octogenarian neighbor was just starting her morning walk through the park and said that she'd get Jenny.

I went back inside, grabbed the phone, and went through my back fence gate into the park, calling for Jenny to come. As for Jenny, she was not interested in coming. She was happily cavorting in her newfound freedom and enjoying all of this unexplored space! A passing jogger saw me and said, "I'll get her," but Jenny, who was focused on the squirrels and birds and new smells, easily evaded everyone's attempts to get close.

There I was at the edge of the bushes in the city park, a mess for all the world to see – red, plaid flannel nightgown, hair disheveled, eyeglasses – phoning to cancel my dental appointment while Jenny moved further into the park.

I closed the gate, went back inside, and threw on some clothes, thinking I'd get into my car and drive around into the park. But when I returned to the kitchen to call Buddy inside, I saw a man peek over the back gate. He asked if I had lost a dog in the park. When I responded "Yes!" he said there was a dog sitting right in front of him. I rushed out to open the gate, but he said, "Wait. Let me get a hold of her collar." It was Jenny, who had been at my house fewer than 24 hours, had never been into the park before, and had never even gone through that gate, yet she had returned to the right spot! Amazing but disconcerting...

I thought long and hard about it: how could I be a good owner to this wonderful dog, when I couldn't even take her for a walk? I would always be concerned that she might escape from the yard while I was away. I had to take her back to Jacquie and give Jenny a chance at a better life with a family more-suited to meeting her exercise and safety needs.

I called Pattie, and we drove again to Jacquie's house. Saying goodbye felt horrible, but I thought I was doing what was in Jenny's best interest.

I cried all the way home. I even bummed a cigarette from Pattie, although I hadn't smoked in years. I just felt such a loss, even though our visit had been short, and even knowing it wasn't a good fit. My heart was broken.

As the week progressed, Jenny never left my mind. Finally, I couldn't stand it anymore, so I called Jacquie from work and said I wanted to bring Jenny to my house "for keeps." But Jacquie had people coming to see Jenny that very afternoon. Oh, no, no, no! I pleaded to Jacquie, "They want *a* Siberian Husky; I want *that* Siberian Husky!"

Jacquie agreed to give me a second chance, so Pattie and I made a third trip to Jacquie's. Woo-hoo! When Jacquie brought Jenny into the living room, Jenny put her two front paws on my shoulders, and we had our big hug, which brings us back to the beginning of this story.

Jenny's re-adoption began a transformation of my side and back yards. I "Siberian-proofed" an existing enclosure in the side yard with a large dog house using concrete curbing and fencing modified to a consistent 7-foot height. I extended the enclosure to include the existing dog door, which gave the dogs a giant, 15-foot by 45-foot secure dog run with access to the house! In the back yard, I heightened the existing fencing with lattice and totally replaced some parts. I also changed the two gates to open *into* the yard, so they could not be "nosed" open if not fully latched.

A funny thing happened while I was in the process of securing the yard for the dogs. Until the updates were complete, whenever I let Jenny into the back yard, I attached her collar to a long lead, which I looped around the leg of a metal and wood patio bench. One Saturday morning, as I sat on the bench with my coffee, enjoying the nice weather, Jenny saw a squirrel run along the fence and jump into a tree. She bolted after it, pulling me *and* the bench halfway across the patio before she realized that she couldn't get to the squirrel! Strong lady!

For a while, a friend's son walked both dogs around the park nearly every day. Then, I bought a three-wheeled scooter, which gave me a renewed ability to walk them myself! A friend wanted to lose weight, so she came over several mornings each week to exercise with us. She and

Buddy would take a leisurely stroll while Jenny and I went as fast as possible, speeding away from them and then zooming back; Jenny got double the distance that Buddy did, and everyone was happy! I was the only one who wasn't out of breath when we came back from our outings.

As Jenny became more relaxed in her new home, I learned how funny and talkative Siberian Huskies can be. Frequently, Jenny would run inside from the back yard, dance around, and "Woo Woo WOO!" to tell me that her Siberian pal, Kiska, had just passed by. She would "Oooh Ooh Oooohhhh!" about our Poodle neighbor, Bono, and "Arrrah Arraaah Arrraha" about that fact that she wanted to go to the park. Right *now*. Jenny especially carried on when the mobile groomer came. As clouds of feather-light, white Siberian undercoat floated out of the van in generous tufts, Jenny howled, "Wooo, Wowoo, Woooh!" as though she was being tortured. I was glad my neighbors had already heard Jenny carry on like that in the yard, so they didn't call to report me for animal abuse!

In the end, I found out that true friends work things out, no matter what, and Jenny and I were friends for life.

 *Nancy Schafhirt*

Northern Nibbles

Magical Maxx: We were enjoying a glass of wine one evening at a pet-friendly hotel, when a young mother approached us with her visually-impaired, two-year-old daughter. Sensing something unusual about the little girl, our recently-adopted Husky, Maxx, did not move, even as the little girl got down on the floor and put her face right into his. We were a little apprehensive, but since Maxx remained calm, and the mother seemed at ease, we just watched as Maxx let her put her face against his. The little girl then got beside him and hugged him. It was one of the sweetest moments we have ever witnessed. The girl's mother said that she had never seen a dog act so sweetly, especially to someone as small as Sophie. The three of us watched in silence as Sophie and Maxx had a magical moment. -*Richard & Virginia Wiggs*

The Husky Highness: Audrey came to us from Norsled after we had to put our other northern-breed dog, Rhen, to sleep. She is a regal, red-and-white Husky. As a youngster of about a year old, she chewed the corner of a speaker, ripped holes in the black mats that covered the hardwood floor, and stole food from the counter tops. When asked about her naughtiness, she looked down her nose at us, as if to say, "I'm the Princess. I can do anything I want." She is named after Audrey Hepburn of Hollywood "royalty." It fits her perfectly! - *Jody Rieder*

Fostering Facts

Alex, our Chow/Shepherd-mix, was 13 years old, and it was time to think about adding a new pup to our pack. She was our first rescued dog.

This time we contacted Siberian Husky Rescue of Florida (SHRF) to adopt our first Husky, Lexi. A couple of months later, seeing that Lexi needed a playmate closer to her age, we adopted Lilli. My daughter was thrilled with Lexi and couldn't believe it when I surprised her with Lilli. Additionally, Lexi and Lilli helped keep Alex's spirit young and active.

Many people think young Huskies are cute and cuddly and don't realize until after the fact how much work they are. That was the case for both Lexi's and Lilli's previous owners, which is how they landed in rescue.

Lexi and Lilli have opposite personalities that complement one another. Lexi is the vocal one who gives us regular updates when we get home. She must greet everyone she meets, and she gets upset with visitors who do not give her ample attention. She can also be an instigator. On the other hand, Lilli just wants to snuggle up and be petted. She also makes sure she gets her fair share of attention from visitors, though she doesn't demand it as loudly as Lexi. Both girls are friendly and playful, thriving on social interaction with people and other dogs. They are my fur-kids, true family members. I can't imagine life without them.

Just when I didn't think there could be a more rewarding experience, I began fostering for SHRF. We have fostered enough dogs now that I believe my girls understand that we are a temporary home for less-fortunate Huskies. They have helped the foster dogs practice social interaction and learn rules and manners (along with an occasional bad habit).

When talking about the prospect of fostering, people often tell me that they don't feel they can foster because they would want to keep all the dogs. The truth is, giving the dogs up *is* difficult, but I just prepare myself by thinking of it more like pet-sitting. Plus, if I kept all of my foster dogs, I would not be able to foster for very long! My house would be exploding with Huskies, which wouldn't be good for anyone. The rescue can only save dogs if there are available foster homes, so the resolve of a foster to let the dogs go is very important.

One rewarding part of fostering for me is seeing the thankful look in a Husky's eyes as he or she comes into my care. It is hard to put into words what I feel when I witness the transformation that some of our foster Huskies go through.

Some have had rougher lives than others, and they are the ones I have the hardest time letting go. My only hope is that none of the Huskies I foster think they had to leave because they did something wrong.

The happiness I see on adopters' faces when they get to add new members to their families is priceless. Hearing updates on how the dogs are doing in their new homes brings a smile to my face. It makes any challenges associated with fostering worthwhile. I'm so proud to be a part of that happiness.

 *Debi Klein*

Chillie's Warmth

Who can forget America's canine media darlings like Rin Tin Tin, Lassie, or even Old Yeller, whose courage and loyalty are burned into our minds as examples of canine love for family? What many don't realize, though, is that outside the movie theater, there are many *real-life* canine heroes. Chillie is one of them.

Chillie woke the Rodriguez family from a sound slumber, not to go out for a walk or to share a warm blanket, but to alert them to a blazing inferno in their New York City apartment.

Because of their loyal companion's heroic efforts, Mr. and Mrs. Rodriguez and their two children were able to escape.

The family's home was unsalvageable, so they found shelter at the Ruth Fernandez Family Residence in the Bronx. With its "no dogs allowed" policy, the family housing complex was not about to give Chillie a hero's welcome. Chillie became the center of a heated legal battle between the Rodriguez family and the New York City shelter. She was the starlet Akita of the city, with Mayor Rudolph Giuliani in her corner asking the housing center to open its doors for the brave canine. Chillie was not only a pet; she was a therapy tool for Mr. Rodriguez, who was recovering from a stroke. Finally, after a lengthy court battle, the shelter permitted the family and their courageous canine to stay, but only temporarily.

Most dogs demonstrating Chillie's heroic qualities would be rewarded with at least a juicy steak, a new toy, and utter devotion. Most owners would face homelessness before relinquishing their beloved pets and would never turn their backs on their best friends. In Chillie's sad case, when it came time for the Rodriguez family to move on, she was rewarded with abandonment and forced to face not only the loss of her family but also the loss of her own life at the notably high-kill Center for Animal Care and Control (CACC) in Manhattan.

Fortunately, Akita Rescue of Western New York (ARWNY) was alerted to Chillie's plight. Our hearts sank when the CACC phoned and described the once-distinguished Akita as depressed and distressed in her cold, hard cell. Shocked and touched by Chillie's story, rescuers and volunteers rallied and brought her to safety.

Following one unsuccessful adoption, we went back to the drawing board for Chillie. Finding a home for an eight-year-old Akita is always challenging because there are many younger Akitas in rescue, and they are all competing for a limited number of adopters. We were all concerned for Chillie's future, but we persevered. Then, one day, fate intervened.

Hogan Sung, a resident of California, was surfing the Internet, trying to build a memorial web page for his deceased Bulldog, coincidentally named Chillie. After typing "Chillie" into a search engine, he stumbled upon ARWNY's website. He read Chillie's story and was convinced that she should become a part of his family.

We brought the two together, but their newfound friendship was soon tested. Most likely from the stress of her ordeal, Chillie bloated, a condition where a dog's stomach twists. Because of her age, the odds were against her, but she pulled through. Hogan selflessly spent everything he had to cover his new friend's surgery.

Many people who were associated with Chillie's story felt that Chillie should be recognized for her heroics. With Hogan's permission, ARWNY submitted Chillie's story to the American Kennel Club's "Awards for Canine Excellence" competition. These awards honor outstanding canines in law enforcement, search and rescue, therapy, service, and exemplary companionship.

The first letter of Chillie's success came to Hogan, and he immediately alerted ARWNY. Chillie was a finalist! She was only one step away from becoming an honorable mention or a winner. The group again waited with fingers (and paws) crossed. Then, we received the news. Chillie had won not only the title but also $1,000 in cash, a beautifully engraved sterling silver collar medallion, and her name on a plaque housed within the AKC Library in New York City!

That year ARWNY raised money to fly Chillie and Hogan to the Akita Nationals, where a ceremony was held to award Chillie with her medallion and other prizes. The AKC's Vice-President, Ronald Rella, presented the award. Mr. Rella told members of ARWNY that he had never been as moved as he was by Chillie's evident devotion to Hogan as she trotted around the ring; it brought tears to his eyes and to the eyes of everyone in the room. Throughout the event, Chillie's eyes never left Hogan's face, conveying the same unconditional love and devotion she had had for her original family, but this time, the feeling was mutual. Many longtime show-people commented about how they could not *pay* to get that look from their show dogs. It was a look of *true* love.

Chillie resided in sunny California with her devoted owner and another more recently adopted Akita named Slash. Hogan happily said, "Chillie is the best dog I've ever had, and I've had some show-quality dogs. Her personality, along with her history, makes her extra-special. Chillie is a fine example of what our breed is truly all about."

For six more years, Chillie's days were filled with walks in the park, friendship, and most of all, love. When Chillie passed on at the advanced age of 14, Hogan had a memorial service for her. She was honorably cremated, and her remains were placed in a special urn at Petrest cemetery, near Chilie the Bulldog and Hogan's Chow.

With tears in his eyes, Hogan said, "Chillie touched everyone as though she were an angel. She was always concerned and giving. Chillie brought me a peace and happiness that I had never experienced before. She had the most expressive eyes, which allowed her to communicate with me. She would sway right to left, as though she were Stevie Wonder. She was an inspiration. Six years with Chillie was too short. "

Chillie's story would not have been told, and she wouldn't have touched the lives she did, were it not for the great group of volunteers at ARWNY and Hogan's willingness to take a chance on a very special old dog.

 *Kathleen DeWees*

Eight-Pack

I have owned dogs all my life, many breeds and many sizes. It was only when my wife and I rescued a purebred Siberian Husky that our lives, as far as dogs go, changed forever.

Nikita (Nikki) was barely two years old when we picked her up from an all-breed rescue in Florida. The moment I spotted her trotting up to us with her tail bouncing, her tongue hanging out of a smiling mouth, and her blue eyes sparkling, I knew we had a keeper. She was not a show dog – her tail was not long enough to curl, and her legs were a little short – but, otherwise, she was a traditional Siberian Husky: black and white with blue eyes and perfect, equilateral-triangle Husky ears.

Nikki was a rambunctious girl who kept us on our toes for a decade. Not long after we first brought her home – I assume to indicate her displeasure at my wife and me for leaving the house for a while – she ate a cloth-covered lounge chair. I do not mean this figuratively. We came home to a chair with *no* covering and *no* stuffing, just a wood frame and some wires. She pooped Dacron stuffing for days.

Nikki was, shall we say, adventurous, to the point of frustration, and we were constantly saying, "No, Nikki. No, Nikki."

We repeated this so much that one of our grandchildren, after spending a short while with us, started calling her "Nonicky," thinking that was her name.

Nikki was a challenge, but I don't want to make it sound like life with our Husky was not enjoyable. Nikki's zest for life and her loyalty and affection had such a profound effect on us that we became volunteers with Siberian Husky Rescue of Florida. We have since happily spent our lives helping to find loving homes for Huskies. Many have found a home with us throughout the years; at present, my wife and I share our lives with six female Siberian Huskies.

Nikki aged in a much healthier fashion than any of our previous or subsequent dogs. Through age 15, her heart remained strong with no murmurs, her lungs stayed clear and healthy, and her sight and hearing were attuned. Of course, she wasn't as healthy as a puppy, but she was as healthy as one can expect an older dog to be.

At 16, her rear legs became weak, and she would slightly drag her back legs when she walked. She must have lost some feeling in the pelvic area because she started having bowel movements without realizing it was happening. Thankfully, our home is almost completely tile, so we had no problems cleaning up after her. After 14-plus years of loyalty to us, Nikki had more than earned the right to be taken care of in her end years. She had spent all those years guarding us and keeping us safe. (We had long ago decided to consider her tightly closed eyes, snoring, and jerking paws as merely diversionary ploys designed to fool potential intruders.)

There were occasions when Nikki had moments of apparent confusion, when she would stand still and look around, as if she were in unfamiliar territory. Yet when her eyes landed on one of us, she would trot over and seem to instantly recognize us. Once she turned 16, Nikki's mobility failed further. She needed help just to get up and stand on our slippery tile floor. She also could not keep up with our five younger girls when we went out walking. I stopped using a leash on her because she wasn't able to go anywhere, even if she had wanted to, and because she would become entangled in the long leashes I had on the other girls. She would follow us down the street relentlessly, until we stopped so she could catch up. When we did stop, she would hop up to us and start jumping up and down on her front legs wanting to play, reminding us of a hoppin' hydraulic Los Angeles low-rider car.

Even at her advanced age, Nikki taught me something that I had never realized before, even though it was as obvious as the sun coming up in the morning. In spite of all her infirmities, she still considered herself to be, and therefore still was, part of the pack. Regardless of her newfound, leash-less freedom, she needed and wanted to be with us. As my wife and I were discussing this need, it dawned on me that the other girls exhibit a similar trait. They always want to be around my wife and me. That was my "Doh!" moment, when I realized that my wife and I do not just have a pack of six female Siberian Huskies; we are as much a part of the pack as any of the dogs. All the indicators of symbiosis are there. *We are a pack of eight!*

When we go away, even for just a few hours, we begin to miss and worry about our girls. At home, wherever we may plop down to sit, we soon hear the clicking of nails on tile, and the room fills up with dogs. When it is time to retire for the night, usually three (sometimes four) of the girls jump into bed with us. They often trade positions during the night, but all six of them sleep somewhere in our bedroom every night. It's like one big cave that the eight of us share.

There is always a parade when Lorraine and I leave the house. The dogs charge the door to the garage hoping that we will let them come with us. When we take them to the dog park, they wander off to do their social butterflicating, but every so often a dog or two will come running back to check in. After a good hug and a pat, they are off, only to return for another check-in 10 minutes later.

I don't know if our girls know that we are not Huskies or that we are not even dogs, but they treat us like one of their own, and we like it. A famous quote by nature and travel writer Edward Hoagland says it all: "In order to really enjoy a dog, one doesn't merely try to train him to be semi-human. The point of it is to open oneself to the possibility of becoming partly a dog."

Nikki taught us to be "partly a dog."

Just 12 days prior to her 17th birthday, Nikki was quietly and peacefully put to sleep, forever to remain in our hearts.

Robert G. Omark

Frenzied Furball

Then & Now

On a weekend excursion to a campground, a volunteer with Siberian Husky Rescue of Florida's (SHRF) spotted Shadow, a four-month-old Husky puppy. Shadow's owner had a lot of questions about the breed, so the volunteer gave her an SHRF business card. The rescue is always happy to answer questions from new Husky parents, as helping owners understand their highly-active furballs is one way to keep these dogs out of shelters.

Unfortunately, in this case, the owner never called. She instead chose to abandon poor Shadow in the cabin in his crate for three days. She left him no food or water, and he was living in his own filth. After the owner did not pay her bill, the campground manager found Shadow along with the business card and a note requesting that Shadow be given to SHRF.

The SHRF volunteer who had previously spoken to Shadow's owner immediately took in this rambunctious, out-of-control, hyper boy. Shadow was wild; he'd had no instruction on how to behave and could run faster than the wind. He was playful and mouthy, typical Husky puppy attributes that would cause shelter workers to label him "unadoptable" and ultimately kill him, had he ended up in a shelter. Thank goodness for SHRF!

I had a six-year-old Siberian, Sitka, at the time and was thinking of adopting a friend for her. She was an alpha female, so I was looking to get a male, and I was not even considering a puppy. Nevertheless, after meeting Shadow and seeing that he needed an experienced Siberian owner who would work with him and help him to become the perfect Siberian boy I knew he could be, I adopted him. I renamed him Niack to give him a fresh start.

The first thing I learned about Niack was that this Houdini boy could escape *every* crate I placed him in, amazingly with no damage to the crate, the house, or his body! It was almost like he would morph out of the crate, leaving it as it was when we placed him in it. As for his mouthing, I soon broke him of his habits with shouts of "Ouch!" each time he mouthed me, telling him in no uncertain terms that his behavior was not acceptable.

Niack drove Sitka crazy. Occasionally Sitak would look at me as if to say, "We are going to return him, right?"

Even so, Sitka learned to love Niack and taught him the "ins and outs" of good Siberian behavior. She also let him know somehow that he now had a *forever* home.

Sitka has since passed on, and the five-month-old Siberian wild child I adopted more than a decade ago is now 13. Niack, my sweet boy, now has two sisters from SHRF, and he continues to have the energy of a two-year-old. (Whoever said they calm down at 10 never met my dog!) I could fill a book with Niack stories like "The Squirrel Incident" and "Mom, I found a Possum," but those are best left for another day. So, in closing, I'd just like to say that even though Niack may have been seen as a "difficult" dog, he became one of the *best* pets in the world. All his "faults" have kept me entertained and always prepared with a funny story! What more could I need?

Nichole Shveima

Nobody Knows

Sammy D came to us four years ago on a sub-zero day, after he had been locked out of his house. His 92-year old dad, Mr. Davis, had suffered a stroke in November and no longer lived at home. On this bitter January morning, Mrs. Davis, in her late 80s, fell and was taken away in an ambulance, leaving Sammy alone in the yard. The Davis' son called me to ask if I would get Sammy.

Sammy's rescue story began earlier that summer on a hot day in June. A caring person saw the big, white dog wandering along a country road and delivered him to a nearby animal hospital, where he was picked up by St. Louis Samoyed Rescue and placed in a boarding kennel to await a home. A few days later, Mr. and Mrs. Davis showed up on my doorstep, looking for a Samoyed to adopt.

    I knew Mr. Davis through our connection with dogs. He loved Samoyeds and had owned a succession of beautiful, white dogs through the years, all named Sammy Davis Jr. I knew that Sammy Davis Jr. III had recently died, but I was surprised when Mr. Davis called to tell me he wanted another dog. Even though Mrs. Davis did not want another dog, Mr. Davis' doctor had recommended that a Sammy was just what her husband needed to keep him out of depression. Normally, we would not have considered placing a dog with such an elderly couple because of concerns about what would happen to the dog when the inevitable happened to the owners, but Mr. Davis had his heart set on it. Since no one had claimed the big, sweet stray in the kennel, and because I lived near enough to the Davis home to keep an eye on the situation, our new rescue became Sammy Davis Jr. IV.

    Calm and quiet, Sammy settled nicely into the Davis' household, as if he knew he had a purpose there. He never chewed on the many items strewn about their home and walked nicely on his leash for Mrs. Davis. Mr. Davis called me often to tell me that Sammy shared his breakfast cereal, that Sammy loved car rides, and that he needed to know whether it was it okay to give Sammy canned tuna juice. He called in November, shortly before the stroke, to tell me, sadly, that he could no longer drive and take Sammy for rides.

    When I went to get Sammy that cold winter morning, he did not want to leave his home; I had a hard time persuading him to get into my car. For the first few weeks, when I took him out on a leash, he wanted to go back toward the Davis' home. Then, Mr. Davis passed away, and unfortunately, Mrs. Davis could not return to her home after her fall. She signed Sammy back to Samoyed Rescue. I had recently lost my beloved Sunny and suddenly realized that I needed Sammy as much as he needed me.

   Nobody knows where this quiet, gentle dog came from, and nobody can say why he came along in time to give a depressed old man a few happy months. Mrs. Davis couldn't have known that after her husband went into the hospital, Sammy D would be her comfort, and I had no way of knowing that he would come into my life just when I needed him.

   Sammy D is a caretaker dog, keeping gentle order among all dogs, cats, and people in his life. He will follow a six-year-old along a fallen log or find a cat who escaped from the house. Naturally, he has become a listening dog for children practicing their reading skills. We have all been blessed to have Sammy D in our lives.

 *Carolyn Herkstroeter*

The ARWNY Seven (Plus Two!)

This New Year's Eve, it will be 10 years since Akita Rescue of Western New York (ARWNY) got the call: a pair of adult Akitas had been abandoned at a shelter in Harlem. The female had given birth to seven pups in the overcrowded shelter, which had no means to handle this litter, let alone two adult Akitas.

The situation was dire. The adults faced euthanasia, and the pups would have no hope. I had a spare bedroom and a small yard, so I offered to foster the mom and pups. Because of my own male Akita, Zeus, I was not able to take in the sire, but ARWNY quickly found an amazing adopter, Jason, to take Tomo. What a relief!

Though I had been fostering with ARWNY for a long time, I had no idea how to raise a day-old litter, but I was willing to do my best. ARWNY helped by contacting top Akita breeders to ask for instructions on raising a newborn litter.

That New Year's Eve, I hopped into the SUV along with my niece, whom I had been "grooming" for rescue, and drove from the Philadelphia area to Harlem to pick up the mom, Sachi, and her puppies. On the way back, I detoured through New Jersey to get a kiddie pool from another volunteer and strap it to the top of the SUV. The pool was necessary for Sachi to have a safe place to raise her pups.

The first few days were not easy. Sachi experienced a major stomach ailment, throwing up daily and having diarrhea. Four of the seven pups were also extremely ill when I picked them up from the shelter. They had pneumonia. The vet said, "Don't count on their survival; focus on the healthier pups."

He said that every four hours I should fill the bathroom with steam, hold each sick pup upside-down by the back legs, and thump their torsos to release the congestion. He underestimated me, I think, as I couldn't let any pups die on my watch! I set the alarm so that every four hours, on the dot, I could treat the sick pups as he had instructed. With our combined determination (those pups definitely wanted to live!), they all healed and thrived.

Suggestions piled in from the Akita breeders, and before long, I had transformed a room that was once wall-to-wall carpet into the perfect puppy training ground. I laid plywood on top of the carpet and put pieces of other types of flooring around, so that the puppies could experience them: tile, linoleum, artificial turf, carpet, and hardwood. I penned-in the baby pool to give the mom and pups a safe place, and inside the pen, I created a "poopy place" from a Rubbermaid under-bed storage bin. I used bricks to create steps in and out so that the pups would not only learn where to potty but also how to climb. (By the time they were adopted at eight weeks old, they were even potty trained!)

In addition to learning all the different surfaces their paws may touch, the pups learned not to be afraid of blenders, vacuums, pots and pans, and other common household noises. I laid PVC sewer piping to create play tunnels so that the pups would not grow up to fear dark spaces and would learn to enjoy challenges. I also built a puppy-sized seesaw in the puppy room.

During the time that I cared for the ARWNY Seven, as we called the puppies, I bonded deeply with Sachi, but Sachi and Zeus did not bond with each other. It was heartbreaking for me to let the pups go, even though I knew they were going to good homes, but it was even more devastating when it came time for Sachi to leave.

I did end up keeping a female pup from the litter, Tasu. Her full name in Japanese is Tasukaru, which means "to be saved," "to be rescued," or "to survive." Appropriate, I thought, for this little lady.

Tasu went on to earn her Canine Good Citizen (CGC) and therapy dog certification (TDI). She has brought extreme joy to many people. She lives in the most historic district of

Philadelphia, and tourists stop daily to discuss her breed and her beauty. They often have Tasu pose for pictures with their tour groups. When the Japanese tourists see her, they respond with reverence and say, "Aah... Akita inu" ("inu" means "dog" in Japanese). They pose for many pictures, but they never ask her to do tricks because they recognize the nobility of this breed. They are always shocked when I explain how she had been left to die at one day old.

Tasu touches lives every day in Philadelphia, which gives me a chance to educate people about a breed that few people encounter and about rescue in general. Tasu even worked on the Obama campaign. There are pictures of her behind police lines, getting crowds excited. She loved the attention and hammed it up. We joke that she should run for mayor!

In order to become the wonderful breed ambassador she is today, Tasu has overcome many obstacles, including bloat, stomach tacking, and ACL surgeries on both rear knees, not to mention the challenges life presented during her first few days on this earth.

I still think about Sachi, but her rescue story has a very happy ending. Jason decided to adopt her, too, after all the pups had found their forever homes. He wanted to give her and Tomo the opportunity to be together for the rest of their lives.

It is not often in rescue that we can give new hope to so many dogs from one family, but this time we got a special chance to affect many lives, both human and canine. Seeing the pictures of Sachi reunited with Tomo and reading their happy stories from Jason and his family, in addition to the joy all the puppies have brought to their new homes (including my own), made it all worth the emotional ups and downs of helping the ARWNY Seven (plus two!).

Heather Hauser Steiner

Northern Nibbles

Spicing Up His Life: My would-be husband adopted Cinnamon from NorSled a few days after we first met. Eight months later we decided to get a companion for her. As a puppy, Cinnamon had never been properly socialized, so she was standoffish with other dogs. That is, before we introduced her to Akino. The second they met, Cinnamon became a bouncing, happy puppy. She was even protective of him when other female dogs approached. Akino really brought out the dog in Cinnamon. Before Akino, Cinnamon slept by the door and didn't know how to play. Nowadays, when Akino walks up to her, pulls on her ear, and harasses her, just like all little brothers do to annoy their sisters, she responds in a playful manner. When he is done, he plops down beside her (almost on top of her) and looks at her with a big, wide grin, as if to say, "I love you!" We may have rescued Akino, but I think he helped rescue Cinnamon, too. -*Laura Brawders*

Never Give Up: Eight-month-old "Mad" Max was the first dog I adopted through a rescue group. This puppy mill-bred Siberian Husky had been purchased from a disreputable pet store, and his owner "could not handle" him. I took him in, and he quickly began to destroy my house *and* leap into my heart. Max had epilepsy and developed bad arthritis in his back at the early age of six, but he is still managing. Despite the challenges, I never gave up on him, not once. We even went through obedience school *twice,* where *I* eventually learned a few things myself! - *Lori Shepard*

Sleeping Beauty

For years, I have been a rescue and adoption coordinator for an active, successful northern-breed rescue group in the Bay Area of California called Northern California Sleddog Rescue (NorSled), so, naturally, when I see a shelter posting about a Husky, I take note.

When I saw Skky's picture from a Los Angeles shelter posting, I was especially moved. Even though this beautiful little girl still had her eyes, she was blind and in significant pain from extreme glaucoma. When I inquired further, I found out that Skky had been dumped at the shelter because the owners "were moving," but I knew that, of course, this was not the real reason. Skky deserved better.

I could not get her out of my head, so I decided to try to arrange transport for Skky from Los Angeles to our organization in the north. Through my many wonderful rescue contacts, I managed to have Skky transported to the Bay Area, which was a miracle in itself because Skky was considered unadoptable and was on the euthanasia list because she needed expensive surgery to have her eyes removed (there was no other "cure").

I could tell when I met Skky that she was a special spirit. She reminded me of a Roomba automatic vacuum, rebounding off things and then continuing in a completely different direction, undaunted. Despite being in awful pain from her disease, she still wanted to be with people, loved to be petted, and was quite curious.

I took her to an eye specialist who said that the pressure in one of her eyes was more than 10 times the normal pressure. I could only imagine the excruciating pain she was in, so I immediately started fundraising for this amazing dog's bilateral enucleation surgery and lined up a foster home for her post-surgery recovery. Then, after two courageous days at my home, Skky was ready for surgery. The vet shaved circles around each eye, which made her look like she was wearing a mask. She sailed through surgery and made some good friends at the specialist's office along the way.

As fate would have it, the foster home I had arranged for her could not keep her, so Skky stayed with me and my five other dogs during her recovery. She and I bonded beautifully, and everyone wanted to know if I was keeping her. "No, absolutely not," I would say emphatically. "I already have five dogs and a busy rescue job. "

As time went on, I started taking Skky to the huge, off-leash dog park with my other dogs. As soon as I released her from her leash, she would run through the tall grass and dig for gophers. (She will get one yet, I'm sure!) She became a sensation with dog lovers, and everyone always asked for her.

After a few months, I realized I would be unable to give up Skky, even if the ideal family came along. She fit too perfectly with my life, and we had become extremely close.

Skky's eye sockets have since healed, and her fur has grown back. She looks beautiful, like she is sleeping (or maybe sleep-walking) all the time. She has a special place in my office, behind a chair next to the door, where she feels safe to rest. She is the first one to greet me at the door when I come home, jumping around happily to welcome me back. She has taught herself directions in the house, and we are working on mushing commands when she's off leash. Of course, since Skky *is* a Husky, she often gets carried away at the park and decides to keep playing, despite my "gee" and "haw" and "good girl" commands. Early on she showed me in no uncertain terms that I should please not try to help her into her special co-pilot passenger seat of my truck; she can jump in quite well on her own, thank you very much.

Skky is learning about kitchen smells and becoming quite a foodie, always in the kitchen when we are cooking. She loves sardines on her kibble, and they have made her coat smooth and shiny (she was not in good shape when she came into rescue).

This dog is my inspiration and friend in rescue. Through her amazing attitude and example, I have gained more courage and fearlessness, and now I feel compelled to always take on the challenging dogs. Who knows if they might turn out to be another Skky-Zoom? She was so worth saving, my special companion.

Thank you, Skky, for everything you have done for me. You truly see with your heart.

 *Gail de Rita*

Compañeros

My wife and I were companions with a beautiful white German Shepherd, Tess, who died a decade ago. After a year of grief, we went to the local SPCA "just to look" and immediately fell in love with a small, mostly-white Siberian Husky, who jumped up in her cage, smiling. At 25 pounds, she was as skinny as a rail from being on the streets. My wife named her "Chula," Spanish for "pretty girl."

    Chula immediately became friends with our other dog, a big Husky/Chow/Akita-mix. They played hard. Chula got knocked around but always squirmed away and jumped back up at the bigger dog. Chula would run away if she got the chance, and once, when she was pretty far into a meadow, her friend ran after her and herded her until I could get there.

When my wife died at home from ALS, Chula jumped up on her death bed and kissed her mouth. When her companion dog died two years later, Chula became very upset, so much so that I knew I had to get her a new friend. That's how I came to have Rico, a mostly-black Husky from Northern California Sled Dog Rescue (NorSled). The pair loved running together with me and play-fighting.

Once, Chula found an old baseball and unbeknownst to me, chewed off the cover and swallowed it, together with some attached material. It became stuck in her stomach and the upper part of her intestine, and it was hard for the vet to diagnose it. She almost died, and I was overwhelmed by the possibility of facing yet another death. A specialist finally figured out what had happened and saved Chula's life by operating on her. More than a foot of her intestine had died and had to be removed, but she recovered and is now as good as new!

Then, last year, I saw on NorSled's list a beautiful, reddish-brown-and-white youngster. I took Rico and Chula to meet her, and we just had to include her in the pack. I named her "Belle," which is French for "pretty woman," to match my Spanish Chula and regal Rico, also a Spanish male name. They all have very different personalities. Chula is a complete pacifist, sweet and always smiling. Rico takes care of the other two and always wants to be petted by everyone. Belle is a bit hyper and vocal. All three love each other and me. They don't try to eat each other's food, and they all respect where the others sleep. As soon as the sun rises, the three of them pounce on me to wake me up, and Chula gives me a gentle kiss on my lips, which does the trick.

Belle runs like mad. Recently, at a big dog park, she ran into the street, and after an encounter with a cop, she can no longer run free. We are adjusting, but I might engage in some civil disobedience when there are no cops around.

When I am out with these three colorful dogs, or when they are in my front yard, people stop and exclaim how beautiful they are. This happens many times each day. They help me cope with the absence of my wife. I couldn't make it without them.

 *Barry Sheppard*

Margun and the Wolf

Decades ago we were adopted by a black-and-white, brown-eyed Siberian Husky who was barely out of puppyhood. She picked us out at Pennsylvania's York County SPCA. We had gone there looking for a smaller dog, but having had a previous acquaintance with a friend's Siberian, we fell for her, and she insisted on following us home. We named her Spica after her origin (the SPCA) and after a star in the constellation Virgo.

Shortly thereafter, my husband, a professor of mathematics at the Penn State University branch campus in York, received an invitation to spend two years at the Institute for Advanced Study (IAS) in Princeton, New Jersey. The IAS is an international, high-powered academic think tank, and we were thrilled to get a chance to spend time there. Neighbors immediately asked, "But what are you going to do with the dog?"

What did they mean, what were we going to do with her? Spica was going with us. We wouldn't have even thought otherwise. The housing for scholars at the IAS permitted pets, and many people brought them along for the year or two they spent studying and doing research there.

Not long after we moved into the ground-floor apartment that the Institute had considerately provided for us to accommodate our dog, we began to hear rumors of a wolf living in the housing area. We were interested and inquired where the wolf lived. They described our apartment. Our Siberian Husky was the "wolf!"

This was highly amusing because Spica was determinedly charming everyone who walked by our apartment: the octogenarian, world-renowned historian of mathematics, who stopped to pet her on his way to and from his office every morning and evening; the scholar father across the street, who brought his toddler over to pet her every day and swore he was going to adopt a brown-eyed Husky when he returned home; and, most of all, the cadre of school children who either lined up or formed a circle around her as they piled off the bus, competing to see who could pet her first. I was the one in the dog house if I didn't have her outside to await the school bus every day. She adored those kids, and they returned the sentiment.

One evening at a party, the young wife of one of the visiting scholars came up to me and said, "I have been meaning to thank you for what your dog has done for my son."

The family was Polish, and young Margun had been having some trouble fitting in because his English was not yet very good. He was shy and diffident, and the other children had not been particularly welcoming.

His mom went on, "Margun has always been just terrified of dogs...all dogs."

"Wait a minute," I interrupted, "Margun is the first one off the bus to run up and pet Spica every day."

"Yes," she said, "And that is the miracle. Margun loves that dog. He is the one who convinced the school bus driver to change where the bus stops, so the kids can all go by her when they get off the bus. It used to stop on the opposite side of the housing, but now it comes all the way around before stopping."

We believe that the other children, as part of their teasing of Margun, had learned that Margun was afraid of dogs. We suspect that they had dared him to go up to "the wolf" and pet it. Children can be merciless in their teasing, and we imagine that Margun was facing a hard decision: refuse to pet "the wolf," even though he'd seen the others "bravely" petting her and be teased the rest of his time there, or summon the courage required to do something he dreaded.

Fortunately, Margun was able to find that courage and quell the teasing. He discovered that not all dogs were fearsome; he got the bus driver to make it easier for the rest of the kids to pet Spica, and, suddenly, he began fitting in better, playing more with the others, and feeling much happier.

We were very proud of our "wolf," who has since become a certified therapy dog.

 *Cheryl Dawson*

Radiant Raki

When Deejay, a huge, russet-colored Siberian male, crossed the Rainbow Bridge after a brief and rather unexpected illness, our female Siberian clearly showed signs of being somewhat disconcerted. Laika, whom we had named after the famed Soviet space dog (Sputnik II, November 3, 1957), was used to sharing the home with the gentle giant.

Accordingly, we began thinking about getting her a companion. Although my experience with Siberians was somewhat limited at that time, since my former dogs had been Malamutes, I was passionate about the breed. Their common ancestry with Canis Lupus (wolves) had me particularly intrigued because, in my undergraduate days, I had been interested in animal behavior and especially the work of famed Austrian, Conrad Lorenz, on wolf imprinting. That study had directed my attention to wolf-descended Spitz-type dogs (Siberians, Malamutes, Samoyeds, American Eskimo Dogs, etc.).

Deejay's breeder suggested we adopt a dog from rescue, as opposed to getting another puppy. It sounded like good advice, so we contacted Northern California Sled Dog Rescue (NorSled). We were amazed at all the wonderful Huskies in their charge who needed forever homes.

Shortly after I contacted NorSled, my attention was drawn to a six-year-old, black-and-white Siberian male named Cherokee. Cherokee was glowingly described as a 60-pound boy who was both playful and controlled, good with other dogs, well-behaved, affectionate (but not possessive), and leash-trained. An outdoor dog all his life, Cherokee had ended up at a Yuba County shelter three times for reasons unknown, since he was not a fence jumper or a digger, according to NorSled's description. After the third time, his previous owner apparently decided that he wasn't worth the impound retrieval fees, so she surrendered him to the shelter.

"Unbelievable!" I thought, as I read more about Cherokee, who seemed to be a wonderful dog by all accounts. So one hot and dusty summer afternoon, I drove up to Yuba City from Sacramento to meet Cherokee. Somewhat mysteriously, I had been warned not to be put off by his appearance, and when his foster mom opened the door, I immediately saw why: Cherokee's former owner had shaved off all his hair! Poor Cherokee looked at with me with what can only be described as a wistfully perplexed doggy expression that clearly said, "This is *so* embarrassing!"

Cherokee's previous owner clearly knew absolutely nothing about the breed, and since the Sacramento Valley is typically extremely hot during the summer, she must have thought that she was doing Cherokee a favor by giving him a whole-body buzz cut to stay cool! I admit it was quite startling to see a nearly-bald Siberian, but the Yuba County area is full of eccentrics and "colorful" characters, so anything is possible up there (even "scalped" Siberian Huskies with Native American names).

What really struck me about Cherokee was the fact that I sensed a strong chemistry between us almost at first sight. His "nakedness" didn't bother me, and while we gazed at each other, I felt a palpable intensity in his look. My instincts immediately informed me that this dog had inner depths of character and great potential as a loving companion. Cherokee was, needless to say, as good as adopted at that moment.

My wife and I decided to rename Cherokee "Raki," a Japanese name (also a strong, anise-flavored Turkish liquor, but that was not what we were thinking of). My study of Lupus dogs had convinced me that the best canine names are short and simple, with no more than two syllables; hence, Raki was perfect, not just for that reason but also because it included the last strong-sounding syllable of his former name. Raki took to his new name quickly, just as he did to everything to which he was introduced.

Our only regret with Raki was that his health was not as solid as his personality, and it broke our hearts to watch him suffer. When he was diagnosed with brittle ketone acidosis, a complex form of diabetes, we began insulin therapy, which required twice-daily injections. Though this is not something most dogs would readily accommodate, Raki tolerated the regimen stoically and suffered nobly without protest. When he later had a large, non-cancerous lesion removed from his leg, he patiently let me change his dressings without any attempt to guard the wound. Although he was also losing his sight due to intractable bilateral cataracts, it was only when Raki suffered a seizure, which left him immobile, that we felt the only humane recourse was to let wonderful Raki depart over the Rainbow Bridge to end his suffering.

On Raki's last day, I remained at his side, silently saying goodbye with my hand on his fur until it was time. Finally, we went to the veterinarian's office, and our veterinarian, a wonderful woman with true affection for dogs, administered the IV injection that would send Raki on his final journey. As I sat there, holding his big head in my hands, Raki gave me a final lick. Soon, his eyes closed gently, and Dr. G affirmed his passing. I'll never forget her eloquence, as she faced us and described the gradually slowing heartbeat she had been listening to: "It was as if he just got up and quietly and peacefully padded away from us..."

To say I still miss wonderful Raki eight years after he passed is the utter truth. I can't even write about him now without tearing up a little at the memory of what a loyal, loving, and utterly trusting guy he was!

Raki stayed with us for four years before we had to let him go. During those four years, he established a place for himself in my affections that no dog will ever equal. I couldn't have known when I first saw that glowing description of "Cherokee" on the NorSled website that it was a gross understatement; Raki was truly radiant.

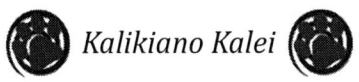 *Kalikiano Kalei*

Sometimes They Choose Us

It was early summer, and we had just recently lost Sedona, our white German Shepherd. Sedona had held a special place in my heart, so I planned not to get another dog for a while. Therefore, my wife and I thought we would instead help some needy animals during the next few months by fostering and evaluating dogs in local shelters for Garden State German Shepherd Rescue.

The closest shelter, Newark Animal Shelter, is a foreboding place located in the heart of the former industrial section of Newark, across from the airport and adjacent to the Amtrak rail lines and a recycling center. Barbed wire surrounds the top of the two-story brick building, and those of us in rescue joke with dark humor that it is there to keep the dogs from making a jail break. Inside are two kennel areas, the first with about 50 runs to a side. When you enter the area, the dogs are usually subdued, but as you start walking down the aisle, the first dog notices you, and then slowly everyone starts perking up and barking. Once a dog is taken out for "the walk to freedom," all heck breaks loose, like a prisoner is getting parole; they all try to get your attention. So, unless you have a specific dog in mind, it is often very hard for any dog to stand out among the din of noise and controlled chaos.

Although I was specifically looking for German Shepherds to evaluate, I tried to keep an eye out for dogs who could go to other rescue groups where I had contacts. For two months, as I did the freedom walk with various Shepherds, there was always one guy who had a knack for catching my eye. He was a unique, tan-ish Husky, who had a spark in his eye and a friendly smile. He always jumped for me when I walked by.

Despite the difficult environment, the shelter staff are always helpful and informative. I developed a good rapport with the onsite manager, so one day we talked about this unusual-looking Husky, whom they had aptly named Hickory for his coloring. Found as a stray, Hickory had already been at the shelter for two months prior to my first seeing him. I couldn't resist taking him for walks every time I came, and it seemed like he knew I was coming, because by the time I got to his run, he would be standing on his hind legs with his tail wagging happily.

It was incredible to me that not only had he been a stray, but, now, going on four months, Hickory still had no takers. I let the shelter know that when I got back from vacation, if he was still there, I would pull him. I contacted Tails of the

Tundra, a northeast Husky rescue, and they approved me as a foster parent. Sure enough, when I returned from vacation, Hickory was waiting for me.

It was the end of August, and Hickory had finally been paroled. After a quick tour of the house, he seemed satisfied and demonstrated his best behavior. It was almost too good to be true, since he didn't even poop *outside* until the fourth day, no matter how long a walk we took. I kept checking the house for surprises, but there were none. He was a perfect gentleman. Even after the three-week period, when the good manners usually start to slide, and we begin the testing phase for new dogs, he didn't counter-surf or jump on furniture. By week six, he had worked his charms, and it was inevitable that my wife and I would fail at fostering.

Having secured his spot in our home, Hickory did start showing us some of his idiosyncrasies. The first came when we decided to foster Princess, a female German Shepherd. Princess was the mother hen, and Hickory wanted none of it. He bulldozed his way past her to get out the door first and constantly enjoyed life "too much," to her displeasure. A few days into our fostering of Princess, Hickory, who until this time had had but one accident in the house, decided to show his displeasure at the situation by looking directly at us, lifting his leg, and peeing on the wall. He only did it once, just to remind us that he was here first, and this was *his* home.

Hickory also developed a quirk with regard to all the rooms without carpeting. At first, we thought he was just a little leery of the kitchen for some reason. However, as time went on, we noticed that he continued to slink into the kitchen until he got comfortable, at which time he would stand up straight and eat. Instead of turning around and walking out, he insisted on backing out of the kitchen until he got onto the carpet, where he returned to walking forward.

We noticed the same quirk once we allowed him in the bedroom, which had wood floors. He slowly walked into the room, turned around at the bed, and then slept beside it. In the morning, he got up, walked backward away from the bed, walked forward toward the door, turned around, and then backed out of the door. No matter how we tried to have him walk straight, he wanted to walk out backward, and he still follows the same process to this day!

Sometimes rescue dogs don't bark for a long time. Hickory didn't seem to have an issue, although we didn't hear a good Husky howl until we'd had him for about six months, and even then, it wasn't really a howl. Then, one night after work, the house phone rang as I was walking up the driveway. As I tried to hustle it up to the front door, I heard this slow "Woo, woo, woo." It then started to build up into a crescendo of a "Woo, woo, woo" Husky howls until it finally reached a full-blown Husky *HOWL*! No matter how much you howl with Hickory, he won't do it, but if he thinks no one is home and the phone rings, he will work his way up to the real thing.

Through four other foster dogs, countless fundraising events, and many sessions helping temperament test other shelter dogs, Hickory's tail continues to wag, his disposition remains easy, and his mouth never fails to smile. It is hard to envision how he was passed by so many times at the shelter, but we are glad he chose us.

 *James Dascoli*

Northern Nibbles

Siberian Strength: Over the course of a decade, Kelsey suffered more than any dog ever should, yet he remained strong, stubborn, and courageous. Disaster struck; our home burned down. When we finally got settled back in, Kelsey started having seizures. He was put on potassium bromide, but the seizures continued. He had a tooth surgically removed, and they continued. He ate my purse and had *three* operations in three days due to peritonitis (an abdominal inflammation). His chance for survival was less than 10%, but he pulled through. Then came the cancer, with survival requiring that his whole fluffy tail be removed, and he continued having seizures. When Kelsey finally passed 10 years after we had adopted him, I began volunteering with Taysia Blue Siberian Husky Rescue, and we adopted another Siberian. He doesn't replace my sweet Kelsey, but *because of Kelsey*, my heart is ready to love again.
-Cody Bloemker

Occasional Alpha: Timber came into our lives because Max needed a playmate (besides me). Timber was two years old and very sweet. He earned his Pet Therapy certificate through the humane society and then went on to "read" with children in afterschool study programs. The kids read to Timber to improve their reading skills, and he loved every minute! To this day Timber loves all children. The boys are now 10 and 11 years old and settling in to being sweet seniors. I have been truly blessed to have Max and Timber in my life. We have our own pack, where sometimes they even let me be the alpha dog! - *Lori Shepard*

Feared and Fearful

One morning, I received a call from a local shelter telling me about a wolf-hybrid on death row. Unfortunately, our rescue would not take her because she was a hybrid. The shelter worker and I tried hard to get her adopted, but she didn't show well because she was hiding in the back of the cage shivering, scared to death. Apparently she had been found wandering around with a male wolf. I am almost certain they got away from someone that was breeding wolf-hybrids for profit! The male wolf was adopted by a Florida Wolf Sanctuary, but they, too, would not take Mischa because she was a hybrid. Her time was almost up.

I begged the shelter worker to keep her another day, but she still didn't get adopted, so I drove two hours to the shelter to see her. When we met, I was astounded; I have never seen an animal so sad. Everyone was scared of her. I asked if anyone had tried to leash her, and the answer was, "I'm not sure."

Of course, no one would adopt a dog who was so fearful *and* feared; she was doomed.

Or was she? I told my husband we had to take her in and find her a home. Honestly, that was my true intention. I went into her run, and she walked right up to me! I put her on a leash and slowly touched her head. She was a bit skinny, but she seemed fine otherwise.

The shelter would not release her to me unless a rescue would sign for it because she was part wolf. I called three rescues, but nobody wanted to help. I finally successfully begged an acquaintance who ran a rescue to fax in a pick-up request, and the next thing I knew, I was driving home with a wolf-hybrid in the back seat.

Mischa was fine on the way home, but when my husband saw the huge dog in my car, he freaked out a bit. The first thing out of his mouth was, "There is no way we are keeping it!" (He actually said "it"!)

My husband was justifiably scared of her, or, rather, her breed. I, on the other hand, had spent some time in Montana around wolves and knew a lot about their behavior. They are very different from dogs in many ways but alike in a lot of ways, too. Mischa was so scared, pacing back and forth in the house, feeling obviously uncomfortable, and looking for places to hide. We tried to keep her in a giant crate overnight, but she broke out of the "maximum security prison" with almost no effort.

I was scared about how Mischa would react to my other four dogs and even more concerned about the cat! Funny enough, it turned out Mischa was actually afraid of the cat, a fact that the cat quickly came to realize and take advantage of. She would stalk Mischa, which totally freaked her out. It was hilarious!

Mischa seemed to take a special interest in our male Dachshund, Capone. I swear, this mischievous, little dog came straight from hell to our house, but he is cute as a button, so we can never really be mad at him. He and Mischa cuddled up together regularly, and she used him as a safety blanket.

My husband was still leery about her, but I asked him to give her a name (at the time, she was still unnamed). He's the one who came up with Mischa. I was already in love with her, but my husband, he was a different story. I believe Mischa knew this because she seemed to take extra effort to wiggle her way into his heart. She followed him around and lay by his feet. It didn't take long for him to say, "Mischa is not going anywhere!"

With the addition of Mischa, we had five dogs and a cat.

Years have gone by, and Mischa has been a delight the whole time. She is now comfortable in her environment and great with the kids and other pets. She is still timid with strangers and new environments, which is typical of a beta wolf. She is beautiful, with golden eyes that seem to pierce through everything; she stalks you with her eyes, constantly checking her environment, and she still loves Capone, who torments her all the time (to her delight). That's what I call *unconditional love*!

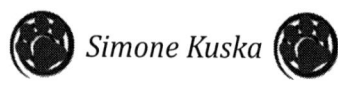 *Simone Kuska*

Sister Sammys

Around the time my yellow Labrador Retriever passed away, Sadie was relinquished to Samoyed Rescue of Utah. She was in terrible condition after having been confined to an outdoor 4' x 4' dirt pen for three or four years. Dorinda, who runs the Utah rescue, spent a lot of time assessing Sadie. The dog was so filthy and matted that it took 11 hours to groom her! (While shaving her may have been the easy way out, it is *never* recommended for a northern-breed dog. If shaved, a northern-breed's undercoat may stop shedding because it lacks the weight to make it fall out, which could result in hair follicles becoming clogged.) Poor Sadie had fungus rotting out her paw pads, and when her paws were washed and cleaned, a lot of the skin came off with the dirt. Since she had never walked on a real surface, the soft, delicate skin couldn't handle the cleaning.

In addition to these issues, Sadie has a scar the size of a soda can on her back. We still do not know where it came from but have speculated that someone may have put a heating pad under her and burned her. The wound has healed, but the fur will never grow back. It's a good thing she's a Samoyed and has plenty of fur to cover it up!

I adopted Sadie right after the rescue took her in. She weighed 90 pounds; she was fat! I put her on a fairly strict diet, and she developed a taste for baked sweet potatoes, carrots, and bananas as snacks. These are still her favorite treats two years later. As her paws began to heal, we started regularly taking short walks, and the pounds melted off. Sadie was even featured in a story about overweight cats and dogs in the Salt Lake Tribune while she was losing weight, and to this day, they still use her cute picture when they are doing features on pets.

Throughout everything, Sadie has been the kindest, gentlest, most loving friend and companion I could ever imagine. She has a level and peaceful temperament, and she loves people. She is a social butterfly and a kid-magnet wherever she goes, and her Samoyed woo-woo-woos sound a lot like she is saying, "I love you."

We had such a good experience with Sadie that when Samoyed Rescue of Utah received Rosie, who was also Sadie's age, we decided that she should become Sadie's sister. Rosie is a retired dog-show champion, who was kept as a pet until her family had a situation where they could no longer have a dog in their home. She and Sadie hit it off right away and have since picked up a lot of each other's fun personality traits.

At first, Rosie was reserved. She looked to Sadie and me for behavioral cues when we would go on adventures together. Nowadays, Rosie loves to dance and do tricks, and every night at dinner she does a little side step, paw over paw, stretch, and bend to celebrate the coming food. Food is not the only thing Rosie likes to put in her mouth, though. She caught a bee during the first week she moved in with us, and she has been obsessed with catching flies and bees ever since. We sometimes have to remove the stingers from her tongue with tweezers! (Good thing she's not allergic!)

Rosie and Sadie are now inseparable. When they decide they want something from me, they gang up, knowing full well that I need them just as much as they need me. (Well, maybe I need them a bit more!) They can usually convince me of their way of thinking.

I love my girls! They are a huge part of our family, and I cannot imagine life being any better than it is with them in it.

Julie Martinez

Our Northern Light

Huddled in a tiny crate with her ears poking through the wires, Aurora was not heading to another dog show where she would prance around the ring, dazzling spectators and judges with her magnificent brindle fur. The colors of her coat coalesced when she ran, evoking images of the northern lights, the aurora borealis, after which she had earned her name. No, this trip was drastically different. Half of her world had gone dark after a capricious romp into an unseen stick resulted in the loss of her left eye. Aurora's ailing owner, unable to care for her, was having her transported to the caring hands of Akita Rescue of Western New York (ARWNY), where she would wait for the one thing she wanted more than winning a blue ribbon: a loving family she could watch over.

My own world had been shrouded in darkness, as my husband and I grieved the recent loss of our female Akita, Roxy, with her littermate, Tomo, mourning at our feet. Through teary eyes, the blurred images of abandoned Akitas on the ARWNY website slowly came into focus. Scrolling, I stopped abruptly; a beautiful, brindle girl instantly captured my heart, pulling the corners of my mouth up in a smile for the first time in weeks. With a few emails and phone calls, the arrangements to adopt her were made.

"Come, Tomo. You're going to meet your new girlfriend!" I called with a gentle tug on his leash.

Ten-year-old Tomo leaped into the back of the SUV, displaying the agility of a much younger dog. My husband, Vinnie, got behind the wheel, and I slipped into the passenger seat, clutching a stuffed toy lamb, a welcoming gift I had bought for my new little girl. When I pressed the belly, the little lamb let out a squeak; Tomo cocked his head from side to side. Raised in our coddling arms since he was a pup, Tomo had grown into a large but gentle adult Akita, alert, dignified, and devoted to his family. There was, however, one renowned Akita characteristic that Tomo lacked – courage! A mama's boy, Tomo could, at times, be afraid of his own shadow, more reminiscent of Scooby Doo than other celebrities more typical of his breed.

We drove south along the New Jersey Turnpike, and the industrial landscape morphed into a more pastoral setting as we trekked 2½ hours from the northeastern-most corner of the state to Carney's Point, nestled in the southwestern tip. I wondered how Aurora would respond to our cuddly coward. The Akita is notoriously intolerant of other dogs, and judging by her photos, Aurora was one hundred percent pure Akita. What if she rejects him?

As we pushed open the screen door to the rescue kennel with Tomo in tow, we were met by the warm, welcoming smile of the kennel owner, Kathy, an individual dedicated to rescuing Akitas young and old, who had lost their homes. Jo, the ARWNY volunteer responsible for fostering and training Aurora, entered the reception area to meet us and discuss the introduction of Tomo and Aurora. "Don't worry about Tomo, he's a big mush." I explained and jokingly added, "He only looks like an Akita!"

Kathy chuckled as she ran her fingers through Tomo's thick coat, admiring him. "Aurora is docile but can be aloof with other dogs." Jo informed us before disappearing through the door leading to the kennels that housed the orphaned Akitas.

My husband stood in the back of the reception area with Tomo, allowing me to greet Aurora first. I inched closer to the door with my heart dancing around in eager anticipation of meeting her. My eyes remained focused on the window in the door, and it seemed as though the clock ticked in slow motion before Jo's dark hair appeared through the opening. Slowly, the door opened, and a black, wet nose poked through. Holding her head high and prancing like a pony, Aurora made her grand entrance. It was as though she knew I was the one who had come for her, and she had called every fiber of her being into action to make herself as pretty and presentable as possible. It was love at first sight for both of us.

With my face stuck in a smile so wide that it hurt, I softly petted her head as she lovingly gazed up. Gently, Aurora took the little lamb toy in her mouth, and her curly tail wagged when Vinnie stroked her head for the first time.

The big moment was now upon us. Jo held Aurora's leash, and Vinnie hung on to Tomo's. Cautiously, the two dogs approached one another. We all held our breath; the only sound was their sniffing. All was going well, but when their muzzles were about a foot apart, we heard a fierce growl backed by a piercing bark. Tomo lunged, showing his teeth! "He is an Akita, after all!" Jo announced, pulling Aurora back to safety.

We made several more attempts to bring the two together. Tomo calmed somewhat, as Aurora stood with her back to him, aloof! Suddenly, Tomo's lip curled, and he charged forward, trying to bite Aurora in the buttocks. Everyone jumped back in shock, especially Aurora. Tomo had found his courage! This wasn't going to work.

As we got back into the car without Aurora, Jo approached, expressing her sorrow that the adoption didn't work out. I held the little lamb up through the window, choking back tears; I had no words. Kathy contacted us a few days later, convinced we were the best family for Aurora, and after a long discussion, we traversed the state once more, this time leaving Tomo home. Fluffed after her bath, Aurora zipped around the front desk at the rescue kennel where I again waited with the little stuffed lamb. Taking the toy in her mouth, Aurora instinctively knew she was going to her forever home and trotted to the front door.

It took a lot of effort, training, and vigilance before Tomo accepted Aurora, but they eventually bonded, and when Tomo passed away, Aurora huddled in the back of her nighttime crate, refusing to come out. She had really fallen for the big lug. I coaxed her out, burying my sobbing face in her soft fur. Aurora helped my husband and me cope with our loss, faithfully remaining at our side. Now she was the one saving us. I later asked Kathy why such a beautiful, loving dog had sat in the rescue shelter for months, passed up by all the potential adopters. Most people didn't want her, Kathy explained, because she was five years old and only had one eye.

Aurora sees more with one eye than most people do with two. With the help of ARWNY, Aurora was given the chance to live and love, and us, to be loved. Every day since we adopted her, Aurora has kept her one eye on us, tracking our every move, loyally watching over her little family. To us, she is as magnificent as any northern lights and truly our guardian angel.

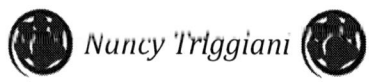

Nancy Triggiani

Akita Angels

Oliver adopted me when he was three years old, and for 10 years, it was just him and me. (My children are grown and live in other states.) Oliver became ill several years ago, but even in the end, his intense Akita loyalty and protective demeanor prevented him from moving on until he sensed I would be all right.

I was able to give my 13-year-old boy that loving reassurance on a Sunday, which also filled me with the inner peace I desperately needed to allow him to progress on. I told Oliver that his love for me would forever remain and protect me as his spirit journeyed to a better place, knowing that we would be together again one day in heaven. Oliver sensed that it was time; he was ready to move on. His eyes communicated an essence of peace as he lay in my arms while I prayed over him at Greenwood Lake Animal Hospital.

Oliver's passing shattered my heart, and a huge void consumed my being. His presence was so powerful; he was so full of love! It was difficult for me to walk around the house without him greeting me around the corners. I couldn't sleep. I just sat in the kitchen where Oliver had spent his last months of life. There were frequent spurts of all-consuming feelings of hurt and loss, followed by endless tears.

Within days of Oliver's passing, as I sat in the kitchen gazing in the direction of where Oliver used to rest, I felt inspired to search the Internet for a rescued Akita. It felt like Oliver was directing me to the website of Akita Rescue of Western New York (ARWNY)! That Friday, just after picking up Oliver's cremated remains, I filled out an ARWNY adoption application for Bert. My application was approved shortly thereafter, and the rest is history! Bert and I have been together now for three years.

If I may, I must brag about my handsome dude. Bert is an intelligent, charismatic, outstanding, gorgeous, lovable, comedic dog! I really think there is a person inside of Bert. (And, no, I'm not "crazy." He just seems so human!) I have regular conversations with Bert, which include discussions of my daily chores and of his brother, Oliver, who brought him into my life. Bert cocks his head as I speak and then communicates through his eyes as if to acknowledge my conversation. I have to watch everything I say. For example,

I was quietly muttering to myself that when I was finished with a particular chore, I wanted to walk him. In seconds, Bert was at the front door, sitting with the leash in his mouth, looking back at me as if to say, "Okay, I'm ready to go out."

My mother and I were laughing the other day because I end up spelling much of my conversation whenever I am talking on the phone with her about Bert's latest adventures. He is gifted with an innate learning ability, and he knows the English language well. I have names for the different rooms in my house, and depending upon which room I want Bert to go into, I will tell him the name. People are amazed; my tone never changes. Bert hears the name and heads straight for that room. Also, before leaving for work, on the days I know that I will be able to walk Bert afterward, I tell him that. Only on those days does he greet me with the leash in his mouth at the front door when I come home.

Oliver would be proud of his little brother. Bert is a certified Bright and Beautiful Therapy Dog and loves visiting and making others happy. He's such a cuddler, thoroughly enjoying snuggling and giving and receiving kisses. He has a distinctive way of communicating warmth and closeness. Bert knows exactly what to do to bring my heart joy, love, and a huge smile! From the moment we rescued each other, we developed a symbiotic bond. Words are not necessary between us in order to understand what the other one is communicating. I just love him to bits, and I make sure that he knows it all the time. I am proud to be an Akita-adopted mommy, first of my angel, Oliver, and now of my precious, heaven-sent Bert.

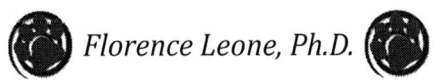 *Florence Leone, Ph.D.*

Déjà Vu

My heart melted at the sight of two pairs of eyes staring up at me from behind metal bars. The sad, crystal-blue eyes seemed desperately pleading, while the lively, brown eyes pumped with adventure, an adventure that I was sadly aware was scheduled to end that day.

I was in Tallahassee, Florida, working at the local animal shelter. These two beautiful Huskies were behind bars for injuring a goat next door when they ventured beyond the confines of their own yard. At the moment, my job was to verify that the dogs in the kennels matched the ones on the list – the list of dogs who, within minutes, would be taking their last breaths.

I quickly crossed off their descriptions and kennel number and asked my supervisor for more information as to why these dogs were worthy of death. She informed me that, due to city policy, no animal that had injured or killed another would be released for adoption. In a desperate effort, I questioned what pack of dogs wouldn't go after a goat given the opportunity and reminded her that purebred Siberian Huskies were highly adoptable.

My supervisor dismissed my arguments, leaving me heartbroken. I recalled my own Siberian Husky, Sapphire's, story of adoption. She had been in a shelter in another county, and because she was infected with heartworms, she was also scheduled to be euthanized. I found her on Petfinder.com after falling in love with the breed and deciding to add one to our family. My husband and I drove three hours to pick her up the same day, and, since then, we have been completely smitten with Siberian Huskies.

The gravity of the current situation pulled me back to Earth, and I quickly began contacting local and national Husky rescue agencies to find one that would share my bleeding heart. Siberian Husky Rescue of Florida (SHRF) returned my call, but the news wasn't great. Although they shared my heart, they didn't have any available foster parents.

I pleaded again with my supervisor to please make an exception. The answer was the same, but this time she "so generously" gave me one extra day to make more contacts.

My work followed me home that night, as it did most nights in my sad occupation. After pouring my heart out to my husband and reminiscing together about Sapphire's life and date with death, he looked over and said to me, "Why don't we foster them?"

Why hadn't I thought of that? Maybe it was because, at that time, we were knee-deep in paperwork to become foster parents through the State of Florida for three children. Regardless, I called SHRF and explained that we were willing to become the dogs' foster parents and find them adoptive homes, if SHRF was able to spring them. They rushed their application and screening process and even worked on the weekend to get us approved as volunteers. Working with SHRF was so easy and pleasant, even though we were a long distance away.

Shortly thereafter, the two beautiful boys got baths and came home with me, but they weren't out of the woods yet. We soon found out that Dash and Steel, as we later named them, were both infected with heartworms. More déjà vu! SHRF quickly organized funds, and the dogs immediately started treatment with a local vet. Over the course of their two-month ordeal, Dash and Steel were a joy to have around, and we took *lots* of pictures and videos. They loved living inside, getting loved on, and pulling our "Florida sled" around the neighborhood.

One day I uploaded two videos to YouTube in order to advertise what a joyful addition these boys would be to any home. The videos quickly hit 1,000 views and put Dash's and Steel's parents-to-be in contact with SHRF. We had a handful of applicants fall through, but then, on the last day of March,

Steel finally made his entrance into his new home. Steel is a big, older boy who is as sweet as pie. At our house, he valued his independence. His new home was absolutely perfect, as it was just Steel and his new dad.

Only four days later, Dash, our beautiful, young, energetic, brown-eyed, adventure-seeker, was placed into an absolutely lovely family of five. He now has many playmates, which include three wonderful children and a brother dog, who is just as goofy as Dash. Given the opportunity, I couldn't have created a more perfect home for either dog.

Both boys are still doing great, and their families adore them. Steel's dad has even become a foster parent for SHRF and has helped several more Huskies find permanent homes. As for me, I am now the mother of five beautiful human children, who were previously foster children, and two canine children. And we are always ready to share our home with any Husky in need!

 *Shannon Carroll*

Northern Nibbles

Second, Best: I'm at an adoption fair, and I see this beautiful, black-and-white Husky with brown eyes. I want her *bad*, but she's so energetic that I almost fall over at least seven times when trying to walk her. The lady helping me says, "Maybe this girl would be better for you?" That's when I meet Kahlua, who does not seem to be interested in me, or in anything, for that matter. She does not move an inch or wag a tail…nothing. I find out that this girl has run away from her owner exactly seven times and has been in rescue for five months. I think, "Ummm… I don't know about this one." Despite my hesitation, I give her a shot, and she becomes the love of my life. Kahlua is a running, high-fiveing, hand-shaking singer! Thank God it did not work out with that other dog. *-Jerica Guidry*

Treasure Trove: With a special-needs daughter, temperament was extremely important when we chose our new dog. Luckily, as a veterinarian who works with rescued dogs, I knew I could trust my friend and client from ARWNY to help guide my choice. We liked Yoshi best, a skinny, lop-eared, fawn male with a sweet expression. When we returned with our children to visit Yoshi one last time before adopting him, he ran around wildly and then came skidding to a halt just in front of my daughter, Paige. He gently lifted his paw to her. If there had been any doubt before, that gesture sealed the deal. Yoshi would definitely have a home with us for life! *-Phyllis Kimmelman, DVM*

Trauma Specialist

Patticake was at least 10 years old and had spent her life in a cage producing puppies. This Husky-mix was not exactly a "puppy mill" dog, but she was about as close as one could get. She had been dumped by her owner when she could not produce enough "profit," and then she had been "adopted" by a sick person who tried to turn her into a vicious guard dog by beating and kicking her until she couldn't walk.

Once rescued, this compact ball of misery just needed a quiet place to die. We decided that because my home is quiet, and since I'm home most of the time due to my age and a disability, Patticake should come to me. When she walked in, she crawled onto a dog bed next to the couch and never moved. I had to coax her outside a few times a day to relieve herself, which was a long process as she hobbled out the door, clearly in great pain. (I live with pain and know it well, so I could easily relate.)

As soon as it was time for her first meal, I started giving Patticake supplements, and after a week or so, her hobbling became noticeably less painful. It also became evident that she did not understand that she could get up and get some water or extra food whenever she wanted. She was so used to confinement that in her mind, the dog bed was her limit. I kept food and water next to her and sat on the couch stroking her. She mostly ignored me and anyone else who came around, remaining quiet in her miserable mental prison.

It took a few weeks and lots of love and supplements, but finally Patticake started walking around. There was a doggie chiropractor who apparently performed miracles, so I started taking Patticake to her regularly. I could literally see her pain diminish!

I had three other dogs at that time: one, an elder whose every day was a gift; the other two, four-year-old girls. Patticake got to see that the other dogs were always treated with love and respect, even if they did something "bad." (One four-year-old's middle name was "Trouble!") When Patticake had been with me for about a month, I took all the dogs to the ocean. As the other dogs ran down the beach in a happy pack, Patti stayed at my side. Suddenly, she started running to keep up with the other dogs. As they trotted along the water's edge, Patticake virtually glowed with joy. She was part of a pack! And they were running on the beach! Free! At one point, Patticake turned and looked at me, and I could see in her eyes it was the best day of her life. That was certainly one of the best moments of mine, too.

Patti has been with me for about 2½ years now. Never in my life has anyone looked at me with the adoration I see in her eyes. Even so, she doesn't enjoy cuddling, although she will tolerate it when I just can't stop myself. She does like to be stroked and to be near, but she only eats in a secluded spot. Patti still doesn't like anyone but me, even after years of love and safety. She barks at everyone and is just beginning to allow folks at the dog park to touch her, which makes me celebrate every time. She will never be "normal," but then again, neither will I!

In our rescue, we always tell people that two dogs are easier than one, and with a traumatized dog, this is the basic truth. Having my other, more secure dogs around has helped immensely. Now I have four other dogs who all, like Patticake, have horror stories from their pasts. There are usually one or more foster dogs, too. I guess you could say my furry helpers and I specialize in traumatized dogs.

It is so rewarding to help a lost soul. They always give me much more than I could ever give them.

 *Jane Eagle*

Winter Wonderland

There are moments that change everything. For me, one of those moments came when I adopted an Akita from a rescue. We already had a female Akita, Mooshki, with terrible separation anxiety, and I thought some company would do her good. When we went to the rescue, our Mooshki was aggressive to all the more "adoptable dogs" that were brought out. As a last ditch effort, they brought out Hobi, a large, heavily-muscled dog, whom they affectionately referred to as "pig dog" for his habit of sticking the entirety of his huge head into food and water bowls at feeding time. Mooshki instantly fell in love.

When we got home with Hobi, we changed his name to Koji. He was a nervous wreck. Although he housetrained easily, his constant pacing and need for attention were unsettling. It got to a point where we would get home from work, take care of our chores, walk the dogs, eat dinner, and then get settled on the bed in hopes that he would quit pacing before midnight. Our patience and persistence with him paid off, and within a couple of months, he had calmed down and realized that he was part of our pack.

Koji and Mooshki went everywhere with me: to work, on family visits, to parks, and on adventures. I purchased dog packs for them so they could carry their own weight on the frequent backpacking trips we took. With Koji's size and strength, he could easily carry more than his share of the load. They accompanied us on trips to Colorado and Wyoming, where we hiked up high into the Rockies for multi-day backcountry backpacking trips. They slept in the tent with us, kept us warm at night, and alerted us whenever wildlife was around. Our Akitas became constant outdoor companions, and Koji and I eventually climbed all 46 of the highest peaks in the Adirondacks together.

The three of us became very close and were quite the spectacle on trails: a big, bearded man with two large Akitas – me with one leash in each hand – all of us wearing backpacks and lumbering down the Appalachian Trail! People were always surprised at how friendly the big working dogs were and how much they seemed to enjoy their work. I even took the dogs on canoeing trips, where they learned to lie down in the canoe and enjoy the ride.

Eventually, I began to think that if I could only train the dogs to pull a sled, we could go on backcountry winter adventures as well. Within a year, I had found harnesses, made a sled, and started the training. The first year was difficult, as I spent a lot of time running in front of the dogs to get them to understand what I wanted. With some help from a local dogsled club, we were off and running and ready to plan our first winter adventures.

In the beginning, I trained the dogs to pull a homemade utility sled loaded with my mountaineering equipment. I would break trail in front of them as we made our way into the backcountry areas of the Adirondacks and Vermont. I would stomp down a trail through the deep snow with snowshoes, and the Akitas would diligently pull the utility sled behind me with all our gear piled high. It was a lot of work, but luckily, the trail we blazed would harden, so I could ride the sled on the way out!

We did many trips in this fashion, and the bond between us became even stronger. In a normal dog/owner relationship, the dog is very dependent upon the owner, looking to that person for food, shelter, fun, and affection. In this new working relationship, *we* became extremely dependent upon *each other*. Once we were deep in the wilderness, I depended on the dogs to pull the load, which was our lifeline. All our food, shelter, and survival gear was in that sled, and without the dogs' strength and endurance, bringing it along would have proved impossible.

Working with Mooshki and Koji in this way made me see them differently. Their determination, trust, and unbelievable strength and spirit became clear, and I started to deeply understand their needs, like when they were tired, bored, or frustrated. Together, we learned how to work with each other, and in the process, we became a close-knit team. As the leader, I came to understand that no matter what, I had to remain calm and upbeat because the team's mood was a reflection of my attitude at all times.

Eventually, I adopted another Akita from rescue, and my addiction to mushing was complete. With this third dog I added a real dogsled and started learning about traditional winter camping and bush craft skills. I purchased a custom canvas tent, complete with a wood stove to warm things up. This warm tent provided good rest and dry clothes in the morning and added comfort that allowed us to lengthen our trips into the winter wilderness.

Traveling with the dogs in winter was great: no bears, no bugs, no snakes, no people, and the entire world was our refrigerator! Because of this, we could bring along fresh meats and luxury items like ice cream. With the strength of a three-dog team, we could easily haul all of this stuff back into our private winter wonderland.

I traveled hundreds of miles in those years with my three furry companions. Since Mooshki, I have been owned by five Akitas, four of whom were from rescue, and all of whom worked like champs on my team. Currently, I maintain a kennel of seven sled dogs of varying breeds, and we continue to work with and learn about each other.

We eventually lost Mooshki from bloat and Koji slowed down after his companion passed. The two had a romance that lasted years, included many adventures, and started me on the path that I still walk today. Koji lived until age 14 and pulled like a maniac until he was 12. That wonderful dog, who was one of the most special to ever own me, was a 100-pound hunk of muscle, fur, and heart. Koji's life accomplishments included the following, in addition to being a trusted companion on the sofa and at the foot of my bed toward the end: hiking to the top of the Colorado Rockies; bagging every high peak in the Adirondacks; pulling a sled for hundreds of miles throughout the Adirondacks, New England, and Canada; receiving his Canine Good Citizen certification; working as a registered therapy dog; modeling for a dog product advertisement; and, last but not least, managing to teach me more about myself than I ever imagined a dog could.

Not too shabby for a "less adoptable" dog!

Chuck Weiss

Matchmaker

Richard stood and pulled me into a bear hug. "Thanks, Doc! I feel like a million bucks!"

Looking down at the dog beside him, he smiled and continued, "And you, my little princess, help me feel that way! You keep me calm, and it's comforting to have you here."

He reached down and scratched Nikka behind her ears. She wagged her tail appreciatively.

"I'll see you next week, then, Richard. Same time."

He moved toward the door, Nikka at his heels. "If I didn't know any better, I'd think she was yours." I called after him.

He turned back to me with a question in his eyes. Anticipating his words I said, "Yes, you can take her out with you. I know she'd enjoy a game of tag."

At my desk, I made several notes about our appointment before checking the clock. Suzanne was notorious for her lack of punctuality, but I thought I'd heard her car pull into the lot earlier. Glancing out the window, I saw that she and Richard were both fussing over Nikka, who was basking in the attention.

I smiled. Richard loved dogs but traveled for work too much to have one. On the other hand, Suzanne had made it clear from our first appointment that *she did not like dogs,* though she eventually learned to like my rescued Akita. This felt like payoff for the long, slow process of rehabilitating Nikka.

Suzanne's relationship with Nikka had evolved slowly. Nikka generally snoozes on her bed in "her" office down the hall while I work with patients, particularly ones like Suzanne who are afraid of or allergic to animals. The day they met, Suzanne had arrived so late for her third appointment that I thought she was a no-show. I had therefore allowed Nikka to return to my office. When Suzanne walked in, I went to return Nikka to "her" office, but Suzanne said, "No, don't put her away. I'm late; I'm sorry. Leave her." Tentatively, at first, they became friends.

Today was different. Suzanne was on time, and she was excited to see Nikka. When the door opened, I said, "I see you met Richard."

"Yeah, I came early because I didn't have to go to the bank. He really likes this dog." She scratched Nikka's chin.

I laughed. "I'm convinced that's why he chose me as his doctor. He likes my dog! What's going on with you?"

Our conversation turned to other subjects.

Two weeks later Suzanne had just left the office when I saw Richard's car pull up. Nikka was immediately alert. He invariably brought along a treat for her, and she was already prancing at the door when I swung it open. She scampered out, dancing merrily about Richard's car. Suzanne laughed and clapped her hands. "What a good dog! Nikka! Here, girl!"

Richard rolled down his window. "She's got another admirer."

"Yes, she sure does! Who wouldn't love this delightful dog?" Suzanne said.

Richard replied, "You know she's on the bad-dog list. She's an Akita."

"Bad dog, shmad dog. This one might lick you to death. I'm allergic to dogs, and the only one I can be around without choking is Nikka. She doesn't smell, she's polite, and she listens to everything I say." Suzanne stroked Nikka's silky head as she spoke.

Richard entered the office, sat down, and said, "Your dog has a fan club."

"What's not to like? She's a really good dog. I'm very lucky."

After those initial encounters, Suzanne and Richard took a few minutes to speak to one another when their appointments aligned. Their chats became longer, and Suzanne made a point of being on time. A month later, Suzanne shyly told me, "I'm having coffee with Richard after this."

"Great! I hope you have a wonderful time, Suzanne."

She looked at me inquiringly. I said, smiling, "No, sorry. Patient confidentiality. I can't tell you one tiny thing about him except that he loves Nikka, and you already know that."

She sighed.

"Just go. Have coffee; have a chat. It'll be good for you. Since Edgar died, you've not been terribly social."

Suzanne dimpled back. "I'll let you know how it goes!"

It went well, I gathered. When Richard entered the office for his next appointment, he smiled broadly when I mentioned that I'd heard they'd enjoyed a snack. "Yep! And we're doing it again this afternoon."

A coffee that day. A walk several days later. Dinner a week after that. Richard told me that they often mentioned Nikka. "She's like our granddaughter, or our goddaughter. We both really love that dog."

Months passed and Richard and Suzanne settled into couple-dom. Dating, frequent phone calls, emails, tweets, texts. As time continued, I weaned them both down to "tune-ups," occasional sessions to keep on track and deal with life's vagaries. Both, however, stopped to visit Nikka when they were in the neighborhood. I'd get a call or a text asking, "If Nikka's free to play, can we take her out?"

Nikka loved these outings. Car trips to the grocery store, walks in the park, games of tag in the yard. She had connected early and intensely to Richard, sensing the angst and uncertainty of his post-traumatic stress disorder (PTSD). During our first sessions, he'd used her as his sounding board, almost ignoring me as he poured out his heart, grief, and anger to my four-legged friend.

Eventually, I told Richard that Nikka had experienced the dog version of PTSD. After being badly abused, starved, and abandoned when her owner's house had burned, she had landed in a high-kill shelter, which is where I had found her. For the first month, she cowered and fled from me. Slowly, we went from fear to tolerance, to acceptance of me *at home*. Moving into the great, wide world and meeting it with interest and enthusiasm took two years, but it was worth every iota of the patience and time it took to turn Nikka into the happy, well-adjusted dog she's become.

I received a call from Richard one day just before Christmas. "Can we both come speak with you? It'll only take a minute."

The pair arrived. They were glowing, and it wasn't just because of the nippy temperatures. "We're getting married!

And we'd love it if Nikka could be part of the wedding, as the ring bearer!"

"You know, the reason we met is because of her." Suzanne said. "I stopped to talk to Richard because he was clearly so fond of her. I've seen bunches of other people in and out of this building, and he's the only one I've spoken with. And it's because of Nikka. So we really want her to be part of our special day. It's important. To both of us."

Reaching over, she took Richard's hand. Beaming, he nodded vigorously.

"She's really great, Doc. It's thanks to her that I've found the love of my life!"

 *Dr. Nancy Almann*

*The names in this story have been changed for privacy purposes.

Pork Chop Pup

After losing one of our four-legged fur babies named Maximus, we needed another dog to fill the huge hole in our hearts. We already had a Siberian Husky named Montana, who, of course, is one of the best dogs in the world. My wife and I knew we wanted another Husky, but where to start?

We found Siberian Husky Rescue of Florida (SHRF) and quickly became convinced that we should rescue one from them. Maybe we'd rescue them all! This would enable us to knit sweaters for everyone in the world. God knows there would be enough fur to go around. There were already plenty of happy baby birds near our yard with a very warm fur nest!

It was hard to see all those beautiful dogs needing homes on the SHRF website. We just did not know how to choose. We went through the adoption process and passed with flying colors. We needed a Husky who would be good with a female dog and with cats. We thought, "This could take a while."

Then, just before Christmas, we received an exciting phone call: "We found a female puppy in your neighborhood!"

We immediately went to look at her. Talk about love at first sight! Kai was absolutely perfect. (Duh, right? Aren't they all?) Oh boy, did she have energy. She was housemates with a Pit Bull, a couple of cats, and a lovely lady named Carly, who, we could tell, gave Kai lots of love. Carly and her roommates just did not have the time to raise another dog, let alone a Husky puppy! We knew Kai would do fine in our home, since she had already had so much exposure to different animals, so that same week we took her for a meet-and-greet with Montana. After the traditional Husky greeting of curly tail waves and a few Husky songs, we were off to a great start. Kai did not pull on the leash nearly as much as Montana did, which made my arms happy and sold me on her right away.

Just in time for Christmas, we were ready to welcome Kai into our home for good. She adjusted quickly, and we see her lying on her back about 90% of the time. We call it "pork chops out" and tell her we wish she could make herself more comfortable.

We also found out that her tongue is both too big and multi-faceted. We have yet to see it stay in her mouth. Her kisses are more like drags of a wet rag on our arms, and I have found her lying on it, as if it were a warm, pink pillow. It is now my alarm clock, too, when she is ready for her 6:00 a.m. morning walk.

Kai's soft, brown eyes remind us our old dog, Maximus, as if he were inside of her, staring at us again. She couldn't have been a more perfect fit. Our cat, Princess, wasn't sold right away, but now, we see her sneak a few "cat love rubs" when she passes by Kai. They are friends, whether she wants to admit it or not.

We did not ask for a puppy in particular, but it sure is fun watching Kai discover new things (well, besides when she digs holes and tears up my plants). Kai loves swimming, hiking for hours, catching lizards (some of which I have had to rescue), camping, and pulling me on rollerblades. She has brought new energy to our older Husky, Montana, though Montana occasionally gives us a look that says, "Really? How much more of this playing can I possibly take?"

Coincidently, Kai's original name was Angel, and to us, she is just that. Along with Montana, she lifts our spirits and brings us love and joy. When we come home from a long day of work, they are both right there to greet us, as if we were the greatest people to ever walk through the front door.

SHRF did a great job connecting a wonderful dog with a family who is grateful to have her. Our hope is that someday needy animals *all* get matched up as perfectly as this.

 *Jared Opalewski*

About Happy Tails Books™

Happy Tails Books™ was created to support animal rescue efforts by showcasing the love and joy adopted dogs have to offer. With the help of animal rescue groups, stories are submitted by people who have adopted dogs, and then Happy Tails Books™ compiles them into breed-specific books. These books serve not only to entertain but also to educate readers about dog adoption and the characteristics of each specific type of dog. Happy Tails Books™ donates a significant portion of proceeds back to the rescue groups that help gather stories for the books.

Happy Tails Books™

To submit a story or learn about other books Happy Tails Books™ publishes, please visit our website at http://happytailsbooks.com.